MAYER SMITH

The Nanny's Billionaire Boss exposed

Copyright © 2025 by Mayer Smith

All rights reserved. No part of this publication may be reproduced, stored or transmitted in any form or by any means, electronic, mechanical, photocopying, recording, scanning, or otherwise without written permission from the publisher. It is illegal to copy this book, post it to a website, or distribute it by any other means without permission.

This novel is entirely a work of fiction. The names, characters and incidents portrayed in it are the work of the author's imagination. Any resemblance to actual persons, living or dead, events or localities is entirely coincidental.

Mayer Smith asserts the moral right to be identified as the author of this work.

Mayer Smith has no responsibility for the persistence or accuracy of URLs for external or third-party Internet Websites referred to in this publication and does not guarantee that any content on such Websites is, or will remain, accurate or appropriate.

Designations used by companies to distinguish their products are often claimed as trademarks. All brand names and product names used in this book and on its cover are trade names, service marks, trademarks and registered trademarks of their respective owners. The publishers and the book are not associated with any product or vendor mentioned in this book. None of the companies referenced within the book have endorsed the book.

First edition

This book was professionally typeset on Reedsy. Find out more at reedsy.com

Contents

1	The Mysterious Job Offer	1
2	The "Driver" and the Child	8
3	A Test of Character	16
4	A Harsh First Impression	25
5	Secrets Behind Mansion Walls	35
6	Unintended Chemistry	44
7	A Night of Vulnerability	53
8	Betrayal and Fury	61
9	A Public Scandal	67
10	The Masquerade Gala	75
11	Betrayal and Fury	83
12	The Masquerade Unmasked	90
13	A Dangerous Game	97
14	The Unraveling	104
15	The Unseen Threat	111
16	Unraveling Threads	118
17	The Breaking Point	125
18	Into the Fire	132
19	The Fall	140
20	The Reckoning	146

One

The Mysterious Job Offer

Sophie Carter exhaled slowly as she stood outside the massive iron gates of the Wolfe estate. The towering structure before her wasn't just a house—it was a fortress. Its dark, regal exterior, the vast grounds stretching beyond the horizon, and the distant flicker of security cameras tracking her movements made it clear: whoever lived here wasn't just rich. They were powerful.

Her fingers trembled slightly as she checked her phone. The address was correct. This was the place.

The wind picked up, rustling her long, honey-blonde hair as she hugged her coat closer to her frame. Nerves twisted in her stomach. She had interviewed for plenty of nanny positions before, but something about this one felt... different.

The job posting had been unusually vague. No details on the employer. Just a single child, six years old, in need of a full-time live-in nanny. High pay, private accommodations, strict confidentiality required. The agency had warned her that the Wolfe family valued their privacy above all else, and if she took this job, she'd be expected to follow their rules without question.

She hadn't hesitated to apply. Sophie needed this. She needed stability—a real job, something that could pull her out of the financial pit she had been stuck in for too long.

Still, something about the secrecy surrounding this position unsettled her. Why the mystery? What kind of family needed a nanny but refused to show their face during the hiring process?

Before she could let the anxiety consume her, a sudden buzz from the intercom startled her.

"Yes?" she said, leaning toward the small speaker embedded in the metal gate.

A male voice crackled through. "Miss Carter?"

She straightened. "Yes, that's me."

"Come in."

With a loud click, the gates parted, opening just enough for her to step inside. The moment she crossed the threshold, they shut behind her with an eerie finality, leaving her no choice but to continue forward.

The driveway was paved in smooth black stone, leading up to a grand entrance where a sleek black SUV idled. As she approached, the back door of the vehicle opened, and a man stepped out.

He wasn't what she expected.

Tall, broad-shouldered, with dark tousled hair and sharp, chiseled features, the man looked more like an actor stepping off a Hollywood set than a driver for a billionaire. His stormy gray eyes fixed on her with an intensity that made her breath hitch, though his expression remained impassive.

"You're Sophie Carter?" His voice was deep, edged with authority.

She nodded. "Yes, sir."

He quirked a brow, as if amused by her formality. "Sir? Do I look that old?"

Sophie swallowed. "I—I just thought—"

His lips twitched, almost as if he wanted to smile but stopped himself. "I'm Daniel," he said instead, offering his hand. "I'll be taking you inside. But first, a couple of ground rules."

Sophie hesitated before shaking his hand. His grip was strong, firm, but not overpowering.

"Ground rules?" she echoed.

"First," he said, stepping back, "You do not ask about Mr. Wolfe. Ever."

Sophie stiffened. "I… won't even meet him?"

Daniel's gaze was unreadable. "If he wants to see you, he'll make that decision. Until then, you're here for Emma. That's your only focus. Understood?"

Her stomach twisted. This was beyond unusual. Most parents were eager to meet their children's caregivers—especially ones who would be living under their roof. But this Mr. Wolfe seemed to want nothing to do with her.

Still, she forced herself to nod. "Understood."

Daniel studied her for a long moment before gesturing to the car. "Get in."

She obeyed, sliding into the backseat, her hands folded tightly in her lap. Daniel climbed into the driver's seat, and the moment the door shut, the locks clicked into place.

Sophie's pulse quickened.

It was just a car. A luxury SUV with tinted windows and leather seats, sure, but just a car. Yet, for some reason, she suddenly felt trapped.

The Mysterious Job Offer

Daniel pulled onto the long, winding driveway, leading them toward the looming estate. Silence filled the cabin, thick and suffocating.

Then, out of nowhere, he asked, "Why did you apply for this job?"

His tone was casual, but something in his voice made Sophie choose her words carefully.

"I love working with children," she said honestly. "And I needed a fresh start."

"A fresh start," he repeated, as if tasting the words. "From what?"

Her throat tightened. "Personal reasons."

A brief pause. Then, to her surprise, Daniel chuckled.

"Smart answer," he murmured.

Sophie frowned. "Excuse me?"

"Most people would have launched into some sob story to make themselves seem more likable. You didn't."

Sophie wasn't sure whether to feel insulted or flattered. "I don't believe in using my past as an audition piece."

His hands tightened on the wheel. "Good."

The car slowed as they neared the front steps of the mansion. A grand entrance loomed ahead—massive doors of polished wood, framed by tall marble pillars.

The car came to a stop, but Daniel didn't immediately get out. Instead, he turned in his seat, his sharp gaze pinning her in place.

"One last thing," he said. "This job isn't easy. Emma… has been through a lot. She doesn't trust people easily. If you're only here for the paycheck, walk away now."

Something in his tone made Sophie's chest tighten. This wasn't just a warning—it was a test.

And for some reason, she got the distinct feeling that Daniel wasn't just a driver.

She met his gaze, steady and unwavering. "I wouldn't be here if I didn't care."

A beat of silence. Then, he nodded.

"Let's go meet Emma."

He climbed out of the car, and Sophie followed, stepping onto the cool stone of the driveway.

As she looked up at the towering mansion before her, a shiver ran down her spine.

The Mysterious Job Offer

Something about this place felt like a trap.

And yet, she couldn't bring herself to turn away.

Not yet.

Two

The "Driver" and the Child

The grand double doors of the Wolfe estate loomed before Sophie, tall and imposing, carved with intricate patterns that spoke of wealth and history. The sheer size of the place made her feel small, insignificant. But she squared her shoulders and followed Daniel up the stone steps, determined not to let the eerie grandeur intimidate her.

Daniel moved with quiet confidence, pulling a keycard from his pocket and swiping it against a sleek panel by the door. With a soft click, the locks disengaged, and the doors swung open.

"Stay close," he said, his voice low.

Sophie hesitated only a moment before stepping inside.

The air was cool, scented faintly with expensive cologne and polished wood. The foyer was a masterpiece—gleaming black marble floors stretched beneath her feet, reflecting the light from an opulent crystal chandelier. A grand staircase curved along the right side of the room, leading to the upper floors, while elegant archways framed the hallways to either side.

But for all its beauty, there was something strangely lifeless about the place.

It was too quiet.

No warmth. No laughter.

No sign that a six-year-old girl lived here at all.

Sophie shivered involuntarily.

Daniel caught the movement and smirked. "Intimidated?"

She lifted her chin. "Should I be?"

His gaze lingered on her for a moment before he turned, gesturing for her to follow. "Come on. Emma's in the sunroom."

They moved down a long corridor, their footsteps muffled by the thick Persian rug beneath them. The mansion was immaculate, but there were no signs of life—no family photos on the walls, no scattered toys or children's drawings pinned to the refrigerator.

Nothing personal.

Just expensive art and furniture that probably cost more than her entire college tuition.

They reached a set of French doors, and Daniel pushed them open, revealing a sun-drenched room lined with floor-to-ceiling windows. Outside, a sprawling garden stretched beyond the glass, with perfectly manicured hedges and a fountain in the center.

But Sophie barely noticed any of it.

Because there, curled up on a window seat with a book in her lap, was Emma Wolfe.

The little girl was tiny, even for six. Her dark curls fell in soft waves around her delicate face, and her blue-gray eyes—so strikingly similar to Daniel's—were downcast, scanning the pages of her book with quiet intensity.

Sophie's heart squeezed.

She looked so alone.

Daniel stepped forward, his voice softer than before. "Emma, someone's here to meet you."

Emma didn't look up immediately. She turned a page, her small fingers tracing the words. Then, after a long moment, she glanced up—her gaze flicking from Daniel to Sophie, wary

The "Driver" and the Child

and unreadable.

Sophie smiled, but Emma didn't return it.

Instead, the girl snapped her book shut and stood, her movements measured, too controlled for a child her age. She wore a neat blue dress, her white socks pulled up to her knees. Not a single wrinkle in her clothing, not a single scuff on her shoes.

Sophie had worked with enough children to recognize the signs.

This was a little girl who had been taught to be perfect.

Emotionless.

Careful.

Sophie took a slow step forward. "Hi, Emma. My name is Sophie."

Emma tilted her head slightly, studying her. "You're the new nanny."

It wasn't a question.

Sophie nodded. "I hope so. I'd love to take care of you—if you'll have me."

Emma blinked, but her expression didn't change. She glanced at Daniel.

"She's staying in the east wing?"

Sophie hesitated, surprised by the maturity in Emma's tone. It was strange, almost unnatural, coming from such a small child.

Daniel nodded. "Yes."

Emma's lips pressed together, as if she were weighing something in her mind. Then, after what felt like forever, she turned back to Sophie.

"You'll leave, too," she said matter-of-factly. "They always do."

The words hit like a punch to the chest.

Sophie's breath caught. "Emma, I—"

"It's okay," the little girl interrupted, her voice quiet but sure. "I don't get attached."

Sophie felt something break inside her.

What had happened to this child to make her so guarded, so convinced that anyone who entered her life would eventually leave?

Before Sophie could respond, Emma turned back toward her book, as if the conversation was already over.

Daniel cleared his throat. "Emma, why don't you show Sophie the garden? I'll be back in a bit."

The "Driver" and the Child

Emma stiffened. "You're leaving?"

Daniel's expression softened for the first time since Sophie had met him. He crouched down, leveling his gaze with Emma's.

"I won't be far," he promised.

The girl hesitated, then nodded. "Okay."

Daniel straightened and glanced at Sophie. "Stay with her. Don't let her out of your sight."

Sophie frowned. "Of course. Is there—"

But before she could finish, Daniel turned and walked out, leaving Sophie alone with the small, silent child who seemed to already believe she would fail her.

The room grew heavy with quiet.

Then, slowly, Emma set her book down and walked toward the garden doors.

Sophie followed.

Outside, the scent of roses and fresh earth filled the air, the garden meticulously arranged into neat pathways and vibrant flower beds. The fountain in the center gurgled softly, the only sound in the otherwise still estate.

Emma walked ahead, her tiny hands clasped behind her back,

her movements graceful, practiced. Like a doll carefully trained to perform.

Sophie hesitated before asking, "Do you like it here?"

Emma stopped, turning slightly. "Do you want the truth, or the answer I'm supposed to give?"

Sophie blinked.

This child.

So young, yet already so guarded.

"The truth," Sophie said softly.

Emma studied her, as if deciding whether or not to believe her. Then, with a small sigh, she sat on the edge of the fountain and said, "It's quiet here."

Sophie sat beside her. "Do you like quiet?"

Emma hesitated, her fingers brushing against the smooth stone. "Sometimes."

Sophie waited, sensing there was more.

Then, in a whisper so soft Sophie almost missed it, Emma added, "But sometimes, it feels like a cage."

A lump formed in Sophie's throat.

The "Driver" and the Child

Before she could speak, a movement in the distance caught her eye.

A shadow.

By the second-floor balcony.

A man.

Tall, dressed in dark slacks and a crisp white shirt, watching them from above.

Sophie's pulse spiked.

Was that—?

But before she could get a clear look, the figure stepped back, disappearing into the shadows.

A shiver ran down her spine.

Something about this place felt off.

And something told her...

That hadn't been a servant.

That had been Mr. Wolfe.

And he had been watching her.

Three

A Test of Character

The shadow on the balcony was gone, but Sophie couldn't shake the sensation of being watched. A prickling unease crawled up her spine as she sat beside Emma by the fountain, her eyes flickering back toward the spot where she had seen the figure. The air seemed thicker now, charged with something unseen.

Had that been Mr. Wolfe?

If so, why hadn't he introduced himself? Why lurk in the shadows, silently observing?

Sophie forced herself to refocus. Emma. The child needed her attention, not her paranoia.

Emma had resumed gazing at the water, her tiny fingers

skimming the surface. There was something deliberate about the way she moved—slow, measured. As if she had been taught to be cautious in everything she did.

Sophie exhaled, choosing her words carefully. "What do you like to do for fun?"

Emma tilted her head slightly, considering the question as if it were a trap.

Finally, she said, "I like reading."

"That's great. What's your favorite book?"

Emma hesitated. "Depends."

"On what?"

"On whether I'm supposed to say something impressive or something I actually like."

Sophie's chest tightened.

This little girl had learned to filter herself, to say what others expected rather than what she truly felt. She was six years old, but she already carried the weight of an adult's self-awareness.

Sophie softened her voice. "I want the real answer."

Emma watched her closely, as if searching for a reason not to trust her. Then, after a long pause, she murmured, "Alice in

Wonderland."

A smile broke across Sophie's face. "That's a beautiful choice."

Emma shrugged. "It's not what I'm supposed to say."

Sophie frowned. "What are you 'supposed' to say?"

Emma straightened her posture, her voice suddenly taking on a formal tone, as if reciting something rehearsed.

"'The Art of War is fascinating, and I also enjoy Shakespeare's tragedies. They teach valuable lessons about power and consequence.'"

Sophie's mouth parted slightly.

Who in the world had taught a six-year-old to answer like that?

"That's…" Sophie struggled to find the right words. "Very sophisticated."

Emma glanced down. "But it's not really true."

"I think the real answer is much better."

Emma looked at her then, searching. It was a quiet moment, heavy with something unspoken.

Then, just as quickly as it came, the vulnerability was gone.

"I should go inside," Emma said abruptly, standing. "I have a piano lesson soon."

Sophie stood as well, adjusting her coat. "Alright. I'll walk you in."

As they moved toward the house, the wind picked up slightly, rustling the leaves. The towering mansion loomed before them, its windows reflecting the overcast sky.

Sophie kept her pace slow beside Emma, resisting the urge to reach for her hand. The girl was still testing her, still deciding if she was worth trusting.

When they reached the back entrance, Daniel was already waiting.

He leaned against the doorframe, arms crossed over his broad chest, his expression unreadable.

Emma immediately stiffened.

Sophie noticed.

"You're back," Emma said, her tone carefully neutral.

Daniel nodded. "Told you I wouldn't be far."

Emma looked as if she wanted to say something else but stopped herself.

Instead, she turned to Sophie. "It was nice meeting you."

The words were polite—mechanical. There was no warmth, no real sentiment behind them.

And then she was gone, slipping through the door without another glance back.

Sophie's stomach twisted as she watched the little girl disappear into the depths of the estate.

The moment she was out of earshot, Sophie turned to Daniel. "She's... not what I expected."

Daniel's expression didn't change. "What did you expect?"

Sophie hesitated. "A child."

Daniel's jaw tightened slightly. "Emma isn't like other kids."

"That much is obvious."

Daniel pushed off the doorframe, his stormy gaze locking onto hers. "You think you know what's best for her already?"

Sophie crossed her arms. "I think a six-year-old should be allowed to talk about Alice in Wonderland without feeling like she's failing some kind of test."

Daniel's lips twitched—just slightly. "She told you about that?"

A Test of Character

Sophie didn't answer.

Daniel exhaled, running a hand through his dark hair. "This job isn't easy. Emma's different. And if you're expecting a typical nanny position, you should probably leave now."

There it was again.

That warning.

A test.

Sophie lifted her chin. "I'm not going anywhere."

Daniel studied her for a long moment. Then, unexpectedly, he smirked.

"Guess we'll see."

He turned and walked away, leaving Sophie standing in the cold.

—-

Sophie's room was on the east wing, as Daniel had mentioned earlier.

A maid had shown her the way after Emma's lesson had started, leading her through more hallways than she could count until they reached a grand door.

"Your suite, Miss Carter," the woman had said before disappearing down the corridor.

Sophie had barely stepped inside before she realized this wasn't a simple guest room.

It was a luxury apartment.

A four-poster bed sat in the center, draped with plush silver and navy bedding. A sitting area with a fireplace and bookshelves lined one wall, and to her left, there was an adjoining bathroom larger than her entire old apartment.

A balcony stretched beyond the French doors at the far end of the room, overlooking the gardens below.

It was too much.

She wasn't used to this.

For a moment, she just stood there, letting it all sink in.

Then, slowly, she moved toward the balcony, pushing the doors open and stepping outside.

The wind was colder here, high up on the estate's second floor.

From here, she could see the whole property—the winding pathways, the elaborate hedges, the fountain where she and Emma had sat earlier.

A Test of Character

And then...

She saw him.

At first, she thought it was Daniel.

But no.

The man standing in the shadows of the garden was different.

His posture, his presence.

He stood by one of the stone archways, half-hidden, watching the house.

Watching her.

Sophie's pulse quickened.

There was something dangerous about the way he stood, like a predator surveying his territory.

Then—he moved.

It was subtle, a shift in stance, but Sophie knew.

He knew she saw him.

Her fingers tightened on the railing.

Her instincts screamed at her to step back, to retreat into the safety of the room.

But she didn't.

She held his gaze, steady and unwavering.

And after what felt like forever, the man turned and disappeared into the night.

Sophie exhaled shakily, her heart hammering against her ribs.

Mr. Wolfe.

She didn't know how she knew.

But she did.

And something told her this was only the beginning.

Four

A Harsh First Impression

The wind had settled into a whisper by the time Sophie forced herself to step back from the balcony. The cold air still clung to her skin, but it was nothing compared to the chill curling in her gut.

Who was he?

The man in the shadows—she had no doubt in her mind. That was Mr. Wolfe.

Why had he been out there, watching her?

And why hadn't he introduced himself like a normal employer?

Sophie closed the balcony doors, locking them out of pure instinct, though she doubted a man like that would need something as simple as a lock to stop him.

A sudden knock on her suite door made her jump.

She swallowed, gathering her breath before opening it.

Daniel stood there, arms crossed, watching her with that same unreadable expression.

"You settling in?" His voice was calm, but there was something too measured about it, as if he were carefully gauging her reaction.

Sophie forced a nod. "The room is... generous."

Daniel let out a quiet chuckle. "It should be. It's bigger than some penthouses in New York."

"Right," she murmured, unable to muster amusement.

Daniel tilted his head slightly. "Something on your mind?"

Sophie hesitated. Should she mention the man in the garden? Would Daniel confirm it was Mr. Wolfe, or would he brush her off?

She decided to test the waters.

"I saw someone outside," she said, keeping her tone casual. "By the archways in the garden."

A Harsh First Impression

Daniel's smirk disappeared instantly.

His entire posture changed—shoulders tightening, arms uncrossing.

For a fraction of a second, there was something almost defensive in his eyes.

"You sure?" His voice was quieter now, slower.

Sophie nodded. "Tall. Dark suit. He was watching the house."

Daniel exhaled through his nose. He didn't look surprised.

"Probably security," he said finally.

Liar.

Sophie knew it wasn't security. She had seen guards when she arrived—men in discreet black suits, stationed at the perimeter. They didn't lurk in the shadows like that. They didn't carry that kind of presence.

But she let it go. For now.

Instead, she changed the subject. "I was just about to go check on Emma."

Daniel nodded. "She's in the library."

Sophie blinked. "Library?"

"You'll get used to it," he said, stepping aside so she could exit. "This place is basically a castle."

Sophie followed him down the halls, the eerie silence of the estate pressing against her ears.

As they walked, she glanced sideways at him. "So, how long have you worked here?"

Daniel didn't immediately answer.

Finally, he said, "A while."

"Are you just the driver?"

The question came out more pointed than she meant, and Daniel actually laughed—a short, rough sound.

"Do I seem like just the driver?"

No. Not at all.

But before she could push further, they reached the library.

It was massive—floor-to-ceiling shelves packed with leather-bound books, a grand chandelier hanging above, and plush chairs scattered across the room.

And there, in the center of it all, sitting at a long wooden table, was Emma.

A Harsh First Impression

She was writing in a notebook, her tiny hand carefully forming letters.

When she heard them enter, she glanced up—but only for a second before returning to her work.

Sophie stepped closer. "Hey, Emma."

Emma didn't respond.

Sophie exchanged a quick glance with Daniel, who simply leaned against the doorway, watching.

"Whatcha working on?" Sophie asked, keeping her tone light.

Emma sighed, as if exhausted by the mere presence of another person. "A lesson."

"Lesson? You have schoolwork already?"

Emma finally looked at her, her blue-gray eyes sharper than before. "I don't go to school. I have private tutors."

Of course she did.

Sophie smiled. "I see. So what's the lesson?"

Emma hesitated.

Then, as if testing her, she turned the notebook so Sophie could see.

The page was filled with cursive sentences, perfectly formed and precise.

But what caught Sophie's attention wasn't the handwriting.

It was the sentence Emma had been writing over and over again.

"Emotions make you weak."

The words twisted something inside Sophie's chest.

Slowly, she looked back at Emma. "Who taught you that?"

Emma blinked. "It's true, isn't it?"

Sophie shook her head. "No. No, it isn't."

Emma frowned, clearly confused.

Before Sophie could say more, another voice cut through the room.

"You're contradicting her lesson, Miss Carter."

The temperature dropped instantly.

Sophie turned slowly.

A man stood in the doorway opposite Daniel.

A Harsh First Impression

And there he was.

Alexander Wolfe.

The man from the garden.

Up close, he was even more intimidating—tall and broad, dressed in a black three-piece suit that looked both effortless and meticulously planned. His dark hair was slicked back, but not perfectly—there was a ruggedness to him, an edge of unrefined control.

But it was his eyes that froze her.

Steely gray. Sharp. Calculating.

And, at that moment, locked directly onto her.

Sophie swallowed.

So this was her employer.

This was the man who had been watching her.

"Mr. Wolfe," she said carefully.

His expression didn't change. "You seem surprised."

Sophie forced herself to hold his gaze. "I was told I wouldn't be meeting you."

A ghost of a smirk flickered across his lips. "Plans change."

Emma immediately straightened in her chair.

Sophie noticed it—the shift.

The way Emma stiffened, her little hands going still, her posture becoming too perfect.

Like a soldier standing at attention.

Like she had been trained to behave a certain way in his presence.

Sophie's stomach twisted.

Alexander stepped further into the room, his presence commanding.

"How is she adjusting?" he asked, but it was clear he wasn't speaking to Sophie.

Emma answered instantly.

"She's fine."

No hesitation. No warmth.

Just fact.

Alexander nodded, his gaze flicking back to Sophie. "And what about you?"

Sophie met his stare evenly. "It's an adjustment."

His smirk returned. "I imagine so."

For a moment, there was silence.

Then, suddenly, Alexander reached out and closed Emma's notebook.

The action was gentle, but final.

"You've written enough for today," he told her.

Emma nodded obediently. "Yes, Father."

Sophie's breath caught.

Father.

Not sir. Not Mr. Wolfe.

Father.

She wasn't sure why it shocked her.

Maybe because the way Emma behaved around him—so stiff, so distant—didn't feel like a little girl talking to her father.

It felt like a student obeying an instructor.

The Nanny's Billionaire Boss exposed

Alexander turned back to Sophie.

For a second, his gaze flickered—down to her hands.

Sophie realized—she had clenched them into fists without noticing.

A slow, knowing smirk curved his lips.

He had seen it.

He had noticed everything.

"Goodnight, Miss Carter," he said smoothly.

And just like that, he turned and walked out.

Emma followed a moment later, leaving Sophie standing in the heavy silence of the library.

Her pulse was racing.

Because in that moment, she had learned something important.

Alexander Wolfe wasn't just wealthy.

He was dangerous.

Five

Secrets Behind Mansion Walls

The weight of Alexander Wolfe's presence still lingered in the air, long after he and Emma had left the library. Sophie stood there, unmoving, her pulse still erratic.

She had known coming into this job that something was off. The secrecy. The strict rules. The eerie stillness of the mansion.

But tonight had confirmed it—this place wasn't just an estate.

It was a prison.

And Emma?

Emma was a prisoner who didn't even know she was locked inside.

Sophie forced herself to inhale slowly, steadying her nerves. There was no use panicking. If she wanted to help Emma, if she wanted to understand what was truly going on here, she had to play smart.

She turned toward Daniel, who was still leaning against the doorway, watching her with an expression that was hard to read.

"You didn't tell me he was home," she said, her voice sharper than she intended.

Daniel shrugged, the faintest smirk touching his lips. "Would it have changed anything?"

Sophie frowned. "Of course it would have. He's my employer. I should have been prepared to meet him."

"You think preparation would've made a difference?" Daniel asked, raising a brow. "No one's ever prepared for Alexander Wolfe."

There was something in his tone—something that sent another chill skittering down Sophie's spine.

"Is he always like that?" she asked carefully.

Daniel's smirk didn't fade, but something in his expression hardened. "Like what?"

Sophie crossed her arms. "Cold. Calculating. Controlling."

Daniel chuckled under his breath. "That's generous. Most people would call him worse."

Sophie studied him. "And what would you call him?"

Daniel's smirk disappeared completely. He tilted his head slightly, as if deciding whether or not to answer. Then, finally, he said, "Someone you don't want as your enemy."

That sent another bolt of unease through her.

Before she could press him further, Daniel pushed off the doorway and nodded toward the hall. "You should get some sleep. Tomorrow's your first full day with Emma, and trust me, you're going to need the rest."

Sophie wanted to argue—wanted to ask more—but she knew Daniel wouldn't give her what she wanted.

Not yet.

So, reluctantly, she exhaled and nodded.

"Goodnight, Daniel."

"Goodnight, Miss Carter," he said, and there was something almost mocking in the way he said her name.

Sophie ignored it and made her way back to her room.

—-

The mansion felt different at night.

The halls were darker, the silence heavier. The dim sconces lining the walls cast long, eerie shadows, and every faint creak of the floorboards made Sophie's heart pound just a little harder.

It felt… haunted.

Not by ghosts.

But by secrets.

When she finally reached her suite, she shut the door quickly behind her, locking it out of instinct.

Her eyes flickered toward the balcony doors.

The memory of the man in the garden—Alexander—watching her from the shadows flashed through her mind.

She crossed the room and yanked the curtains shut.

Then, exhaling, she sat down on the edge of her bed, running her hands through her hair.

This job was turning out to be so much more than she expected.

She had come here thinking she was just going to be a nanny. That she would take care of a little girl, help her open up, teach her things like any normal child.

But Emma wasn't normal.

And this wasn't a normal household.

Sophie knew—deep in her gut—that there was something very, very wrong with this family.

And if she wanted to protect Emma, she had to find out what.

—-

Morning came too quickly.

Sophie had barely gotten any sleep, her mind racing with thoughts of last night. But she forced herself up early, got dressed in comfortable jeans and a simple blouse, and made her way downstairs.

She didn't know exactly where to find Emma, but she had a feeling that, just like last night, she wouldn't find her playing with toys or watching cartoons.

She was right.

Emma was in the piano room.

The moment Sophie stepped inside, she saw the little girl sitting on the piano bench, her small hands pressed perfectly against the ivory keys. A strict-looking woman stood beside her, arms crossed, watching like a hawk.

The woman's sharp eyes flicked toward Sophie the moment she entered.

"You are interrupting a lesson," the woman said curtly.

Sophie ignored her and stepped forward. "Good morning, Emma."

Emma's fingers hovered over the keys, but she didn't respond.

The woman turned fully toward Sophie now, clearly annoyed. "This is a structured environment, Miss Carter. Miss Wolfe follows a very rigorous schedule. If you are to be effective in this household, you will need to learn that."

Sophie held back her irritation.

"And you are?"

The woman straightened. "Mrs. Laurent. I oversee Emma's education."

Sophie nodded, keeping her tone neutral. "Nice to meet you. And what exactly is on the schedule for today?"

"Emma has piano for another hour. Then Latin studies, arithmetic, French, and etiquette."

Sophie's eyebrows lifted. "That's… a lot for a six-year-old."

Mrs. Laurent's lips thinned. "Emma is not an ordinary six-year-old."

Sophie's gaze flickered to Emma, whose eyes were still glued to the piano keys, as if she were trying to disappear into them.

A protective instinct surged inside her.

"Can I have a moment with her?" Sophie asked.

Mrs. Laurent scoffed. "Absolutely not. We do not deviate from—"

"It's fine," Emma interrupted quietly.

Both women turned to look at her.

Emma finally looked up from the piano and met Sophie's gaze.

"I'd like to speak with her alone," she said.

Mrs. Laurent visibly stiffened.

For a moment, she looked like she wanted to argue.

Then, finally, she exhaled sharply. "Fine. But don't waste too much time. We have a schedule to maintain."

With that, she turned on her heel and strode out of the room, leaving Sophie and Emma alone.

For a moment, there was only silence.

Then, Sophie walked over and sat beside Emma on the piano bench.

She glanced at the sheet music in front of them. "Do you like playing?"

Emma shrugged. "I like some songs."

"And the others?"

Emma hesitated.

Then, quietly, she admitted, "They're just for show."

Sophie exhaled. "Do you ever get to play? Just for fun?"

Emma looked away. "Fun doesn't matter here."

Sophie's jaw tightened.

This little girl—this brilliant, observant, guarded little girl—had been trained to see the world in black and white. Performance and failure. Strength and weakness.

She wanted to change that.

She wanted Emma to see that it was okay to be a child.

"You know," Sophie said, tapping a key softly, "Alice in Wonderland has a song in it."

Emma's head tilted slightly. "It does?"

Sophie nodded. "It's called 'Golden Afternoon.' Want to learn it?"

Emma hesitated.

Then, after a long moment, she whispered, "Okay."

Sophie smiled.

It was small—so small it was barely anything at all.

But it was a start.

And Sophie was not going to let Emma become another cold, lifeless piece of this mansion.

Not while she was here.

Six

Unintended Chemistry

The delicate notes of the piano filled the air, soft and uncertain at first, then gradually growing more confident as Emma's small fingers pressed against the keys. Sophie sat beside her, guiding her gently, humming the tune of Golden Afternoon under her breath.

It was a stark contrast to the rigid atmosphere Sophie had felt since stepping into the mansion. For the first time since she arrived, the moment felt real—unscripted, unforced.

Emma's lips parted slightly, her concentration deep as she played.

"You're doing great," Sophie whispered, careful not to break the spell.

Unintended Chemistry

Emma didn't say anything, but her tiny shoulders relaxed just a little.

It was a small victory, but Sophie would take it.

She had barely been here a full day, but she already understood that Emma's world was made up of expectations. Every movement, every word, every decision had been calculated—as if she were afraid of stepping out of line.

Sophie's heart ached for her.

The sound of the door clicking open made Emma instantly stiffen.

The spell was broken.

The music halted.

Sophie turned, expecting to see Mrs. Laurent coming back to enforce another rule.

But instead, she was met with a much darker presence.

Alexander Wolfe.

He stood just inside the room, his tall frame perfectly still, his expression unreadable. He had changed from his suit into something more casual—black slacks and a fitted gray sweater—but the effect was still the same.

Powerful. Intimidating. Unshakable.

His stormy gray eyes flicked over the scene before him, lingering on Emma's hands poised over the keys before settling on Sophie.

"Miss Carter," he said smoothly, his voice like velvet over steel. "I wasn't aware this was part of your duties."

Sophie straightened. "Emma and I were just having a little fun."

Alexander's gaze hardened just slightly. "Emma's schedule is structured for a reason."

Emma's posture was too perfect, her back rigid, her hands carefully resting on her lap. Her expression was blank.

A sharp contrast to the girl who, just seconds ago, had been playing music freely.

Sophie's chest tightened.

"She's still learning," Sophie said, choosing her words carefully. "Just in a different way."

Alexander took a slow step forward. "Is that what you think your job is? To decide how my daughter learns?"

Sophie met his stare head-on. "I think my job is to help her. And from what I've seen, she needs a lot more than just structure."

A silence stretched between them, thick with tension.

Daniel had been right.

No one was ever prepared for Alexander Wolfe.

His presence was crushing, his intensity almost suffocating. He wasn't just a billionaire with influence—he was a man who expected the world to bend to his will.

Sophie could feel the weight of that expectation pressing against her.

But she refused to break.

Finally, Alexander let out a slow breath. "Emma, you're excused."

Emma hesitated for only a second before nodding. "Yes, Father."

She slid off the bench, gave Sophie a fleeting glance, then hurried out of the room without another word.

The door shut behind her, leaving Sophie and Alexander alone.

The air felt heavier now.

Sophie forced herself to hold her ground, despite the way her pulse quickened under Alexander's piercing stare.

He moved closer—slow, deliberate. The faint scent of his cologne drifted in the space between them, a mix of sandalwood and something deeper, something that shouldn't be so distracting.

He stopped just a foot away from her.

Too close.

"Do you have any idea what you're doing?" he asked quietly, but there was no softness in his tone.

Sophie lifted her chin. "I'm helping Emma."

"No," he murmured. "You're interfering."

Sophie's breath caught.

"Emma is not like other children," Alexander continued. "She doesn't need a nanny who will coddle her. She needs discipline. Strength."

"She's six," Sophie shot back. "She needs to be a child."

For a split second, something flickered in Alexander's eyes. A storm of emotion—anger, frustration, maybe something else. But it was gone as quickly as it came.

"She needs to be prepared for the world," he said evenly.

Sophie clenched her jaw. "And what exactly are you preparing her for?"

Alexander's expression didn't change. But there was something cold behind his eyes now, something that sent a chill down Sophie's spine.

A beat of silence passed.

Then, in a voice so low it almost felt like a warning, he said,

"She is my daughter, Miss Carter. You are just an employee."

The words cut through the air like a blade.

Sophie knew what he was doing.

He was establishing control.

Reminding her who held the power in this house.

She had worked for difficult families before—strict, overbearing parents who micromanaged every second of their child's life.

But Alexander Wolfe wasn't just difficult.

He was dangerous.

And yet…

Despite every warning bell in her head, Sophie refused to back down.

She took a slow step forward, closing the gap between them just slightly.

"I may be just an employee," she said softly. "But I'm also the only one here who seems to care that your daughter is hurting."

Something shifted in Alexander's expression.

For the first time, his mask cracked.

It was subtle—so subtle that if Sophie hadn't been watching closely, she might have missed it.

The flicker of hesitation.

The barest flash of guilt.

But just as quickly, it was gone.

Alexander took a slow breath, his jaw tightening.

And then, to Sophie's utter surprise, he smirked.

Not a full smile. Just the faintest curve of his lips.

"Be careful, Miss Carter," he murmured. "You're stepping into territory you don't understand."

The words sent another shiver down her spine.

But she refused to let him see it.

She squared her shoulders. "Then maybe you should explain it to me."

Alexander chuckled—a low, rich sound, full of something dark and unreadable.

"You really aren't afraid of me, are you?"

Sophie swallowed. "Should I be?"

His smirk deepened.

Instead of answering, he took a step back, his gaze still locked onto hers.

Then, without another word, he turned and walked out of the room.

Sophie stood there, heart pounding, her breath uneven.

The tension in the air still sizzled, lingering like an electric current.

She had challenged him.

And instead of firing her on the spot…

He had smiled.

Sophie wasn't sure what was more terrifying—Alexander Wolfe's control…

Or the fact that, for a moment, she had felt something dangerously close to chemistry crackling between them.

Seven

A Night of Vulnerability

The moon hung high in the sky, casting its silvery glow over the sprawling Wolfe estate, but the air inside the mansion was thick with tension. Sophie paced across the floor of her room, running her fingers through her hair as her mind raced with the encounter earlier that evening.

Alexander Wolfe's presence had shaken her in a way that no other employer ever had. His power. His control. His inability to show even a hint of vulnerability. Sophie couldn't stop thinking about that small crack in his armor—the brief flicker of something almost human in his eyes before he had turned and walked away.

She had spent hours lying in bed, unable to sleep, her mind relentlessly replaying their conversation.

What had he meant when he said she was stepping into territory she didn't understand? Was it a warning? Or was there something more to his words?

Sophie had been around people who liked to keep their emotions buried, but Alexander Wolfe... he was a master at it. And yet, she couldn't help but feel like there was more beneath the surface. Something raw and painful that he kept hidden so deeply, even from himself.

A sharp knock on the door pulled her from her thoughts.

Sophie's heart skipped a beat as she hurried to the door, hoping it wasn't Mrs. Laurent coming to check on her or, worse, someone from security telling her she was doing something wrong.

When she opened it, she was met with the last person she expected.

Alexander Wolfe.

He was standing in the doorway, his usual confident posture giving way to something different tonight. His jaw was clenched, his eyes shadowed with an intensity Sophie hadn't seen before. He looked... almost vulnerable.

"Mr. Wolfe?" Sophie asked, her voice catching in her throat.

He didn't respond immediately. Instead, he stepped inside without waiting for an invitation, his presence filling the room in a way that made Sophie's pulse quicken.

"Is something wrong?" Sophie asked, trying to keep her voice steady.

He hesitated, his lips pressed into a thin line. "I need to speak with you."

The words hung in the air between them, and Sophie's instincts flared. This wasn't just a casual conversation. There was something heavy behind his tone.

"Of course," she said, her heart racing. "What's this about?"

He closed the door behind him, his gaze not leaving hers for a moment as if weighing something inside him. Then, finally, he spoke, his voice lower than usual.

"I've been thinking about our conversation earlier."

Sophie's breath caught. He was referring to their exchange in the piano room, where she had dared to challenge him.

"I should have warned you," he continued, his words slow and deliberate, "about what you're getting into here. About my daughter. About me."

Sophie narrowed her eyes. "What do you mean?"

Alexander looked away for a brief moment, running a hand through his hair, his frustration palpable. When he met her gaze again, there was a flicker of something else in his eyes—regret, perhaps, or something deeper, something Sophie couldn't quite place.

"I've been… hard on Emma," he admitted, his voice barely above a whisper. "Not because I want to be, but because I have no choice."

Sophie's breath hitched. "What do you mean, no choice?"

Alexander's gaze turned cold again, but the tightness around his eyes betrayed his emotional struggle. He took a step forward, closing the distance between them.

"Because the world is cold, Sophie," he said quietly. "Because I've seen what happens to people who are soft. To people who don't know how to protect themselves. Emma can't afford to be soft. She can't afford to be like other children. You have no idea what she's up against."

Sophie felt a knot form in her stomach. She had never seen Alexander so raw before, so vulnerable. This wasn't the powerful, unflinching man she had seen in the mansion's halls—this was someone completely different.

"You can't protect her from the world by turning her into something she's not," Sophie said softly. "She needs love, not control. She needs a childhood, not a prison."

The words stung, but they were true.

A Night of Vulnerability

Alexander's expression shifted, a flicker of something almost like guilt crossing his features. He looked away for a moment, the weight of his emotions suddenly too much to bear. Sophie could feel the tension in the room, the unbearable distance between them.

"I know," he murmured, his voice strained. "I know that, Sophie. But it's not that simple. You don't understand the pressures I face. You don't know what it's like to lose everything, to have to rebuild from the ground up. To constantly be on guard, watching your back every second of the day."

Sophie's heart twisted. She could hear the pain in his voice. The weight of a past that he had never shared with anyone, perhaps not even with himself.

She wanted to say something, to comfort him, but the words caught in her throat. She didn't know how. This wasn't the Alexander she knew. The man who had been cold and distant, always in control. This man was vulnerable, a man who had suffered losses that Sophie couldn't even imagine.

"Tell me," she whispered, stepping a little closer, "What happened to you?"

Alexander's eyes flicked to hers, a flicker of hesitation crossing his features. He opened his mouth as if to speak but stopped himself. For a long moment, he was silent, his lips pressed into a thin line, as if he were fighting some inner battle.

Then, finally, he spoke.

"I lost my wife," he said, his voice raw with emotion. "She died when Emma was just a baby. I've spent the last six years trying to protect her from the world that took her mother away."

Sophie's heart broke for him. She had known he had lost someone important, but she hadn't realized just how much it had destroyed him.

"I'm sorry," she said, her voice soft. "I didn't know."

Alexander's gaze softened for a moment, his expression breaking just slightly. But it didn't last. He quickly turned away, his eyes clouding again with something dark and unreadable.

"I don't expect you to understand," he said, his voice low and sharp. "But I will not let Emma become a victim of this world. I will not let her grow up weak."

Sophie's heart ached for him. She could see the battle within him, the conflict between wanting to protect his daughter and pushing her too far.

"But she's not weak," Sophie said gently. "She's strong in her own way, Alexander. You just have to let her be a child first."

Alexander's eyes darkened again, but this time, there was something else there—something fragile that he wasn't willing to let go of.

"You don't know what it's like," he said, his voice colder now. "You don't understand the weight of the decisions I have to make every day. The sacrifices I've had to make to protect her, to keep her safe."

Sophie reached out, placing a hand on his arm. He flinched slightly, but didn't pull away.

"I don't know your struggles, Alexander," she said softly, "But I know one thing. If you push Emma too hard, you'll break her. You'll break both of you."

There was a long silence, the air between them thick with unspoken words. Sophie could feel the pull between them, the intensity of the moment crackling like static in the air. She knew that they were standing on the edge of something—something dangerous, something unavoidable.

And yet, for the first time since meeting him, she felt like she was seeing Alexander clearly. Not just the cold, distant billionaire, but the broken man who had lost so much and was too afraid to let anyone in.

Finally, Alexander exhaled, his chest rising and falling with a deep breath. "I don't know how to fix this," he said, his voice quieter now. "I don't know how to make it right."

Sophie looked up at him, her gaze steady and unwavering. "You're not alone, Alexander. You don't have to do this by yourself."

For a moment, their eyes locked, and Sophie could see the turmoil in his gaze—the fear, the grief, the longing for something he hadn't allowed himself to feel in a long time.

Then, as if he couldn't bear the weight of the moment any longer, he pulled back, stepping away from her with a sharp breath.

"I need to go," he said, his voice suddenly businesslike again. "We'll talk more about this later."

Sophie nodded, though her heart still ached for him. As Alexander turned and walked toward the door, something shifted between them. A fragile understanding, a shared moment of vulnerability.

The door clicked shut behind him, and Sophie stood there in the silence, her hand still resting on her chest.

She had reached him.

But at what cost?

And more importantly, where would it lead?

Eight

Betrayal and Fury

The next morning, the quiet of the mansion felt suffocating. Sophie had barely slept, the weight of the conversation with Alexander from the night before still hanging in her mind. She had learned more than she ever expected to know about him—about his pain, his fear, and the way he tried to control everything around him in an attempt to protect his daughter.

But she hadn't realized that speaking those truths would change things between them, would make him see her differently. She hadn't anticipated that she would pierce his armor, and it left her feeling exposed, like she had taken a step too far.

She stood in front of the mirror, adjusting her blouse, her mind a whirl of thoughts. She should be focusing on Emma, helping her with the lessons, guiding her through the day. But ever since last night, she couldn't help but wonder what would happen next. Could she really continue to play the role of just a nanny when everything had suddenly become so much more personal?

There was a soft knock on the door, followed by the creak of it opening.

"Miss Carter?"

Sophie turned quickly to find Daniel standing in the doorway, his face impassive, but his eyes flickering with something she couldn't quite place.

"Yes?" she asked, trying to mask the tension in her voice.

"I need to speak with you," he said, his tone flat, but his gaze never leaving hers. There was something in his posture that felt urgent, something that made Sophie's instincts flare.

Her heart skipped a beat. "Of course," she replied, setting down the hairbrush she had been holding.

Daniel stepped into the room, the door clicking shut behind him. For a moment, neither of them spoke. Sophie's mind raced, her body tense with anticipation, as if she were waiting for the ground to drop out from beneath her.

Finally, Daniel broke the silence. "You need to be careful," he said in a low voice, his eyes narrowing slightly.

Betrayal and Fury

Sophie frowned. "Careful about what?"

Daniel hesitated, glancing over his shoulder, his voice dropping to a whisper. "About Alexander." His eyes flicked back to her. "You've been… closer than you think to crossing a line."

Sophie's pulse quickened. "What do you mean?" she asked, her words more demanding than she intended.

Daniel stepped forward, lowering his voice even further. "I know what happened last night," he said. "I saw you two talking. I saw the way he was with you." His jaw tightened, his lips pressed into a thin line. "You're treading dangerously, Sophie."

Sophie took a step back, the shock of his words hitting her like a blow to the chest. "What are you talking about? We were just talking."

Daniel shook his head. "It's not just talking, is it? Alexander doesn't let people in. He doesn't show anyone that side of him—ever." His voice was filled with something dark, something Sophie couldn't understand. "And yet, you saw it. You made him open up. You made him feel. That's dangerous."

Sophie's breath hitched. She had suspected that Alexander kept his emotions locked away, but hearing Daniel's words felt like a punch to the gut. She had never meant to cause trouble, never meant to get too close, but something inside her had reached out to him—something about his pain and isolation had resonated with her. She had tried to help him, to understand him, but now… now it felt like she had done something wrong.

"What do you expect me to do?" she asked, her voice strained. "I care about Emma. I care about helping her. But I can't pretend that I don't see what's going on with her father. I can't ignore it." She took a deep breath. "And neither should you."

Daniel's gaze hardened. "You think you know what's going on here?" His voice was bitter, almost mocking. "You don't know anything, Sophie. You don't know who Alexander is. You don't know what he's capable of."

Sophie flinched at the venom in his words, but she refused to back down. "What is he capable of, Daniel? What are you so afraid of?"

He looked away for a moment, his jaw clenched, as if struggling with something. Then, with a deep breath, he spoke, his voice low but laced with anger.

"Alexander Wolfe doesn't let anyone get close to him. Not because he's afraid of feeling—but because when you get too close to him, he destroys you. He does it without even thinking. He'll push you away, and then when you try to leave, he'll destroy everything you've built. He'll tear it all down. And you'll never even see it coming."

Sophie's heart raced as Daniel's words sank in. She didn't know if he was trying to scare her or if he was telling the truth. But the fear in his eyes made her realize that he wasn't just speaking out of bitterness. He genuinely believed what he was saying.

"I'm not afraid of him," Sophie said, her voice steadier than she felt. "But if you're right, then I need to know why. I need to understand why he's like this."

Daniel's eyes locked onto hers, his expression a mixture of frustration and something darker. "You think you can fix him? That you can change him?" He shook his head, almost laughing, though there was no humor in it. "You can't change someone like Alexander. You can't fix what's broken inside him."

Before Sophie could respond, there was a sharp knock on the door.

"Miss Carter," a voice called from the other side. It was Mrs. Laurent, her tone icy. "It's time to begin the day's lessons with Emma."

Sophie glanced at Daniel, her mind a whirl of confusion and fear. He stepped back, nodding toward the door. "I'd be careful if I were you," he muttered, his voice barely audible.

Sophie turned, but before she could open the door, Daniel's hand shot out, stopping her.

"Whatever you think you're doing, Sophie, stop. Just stop. You have no idea what you're dealing with."

He spun on his heel and left the room, the door clicking shut behind him.

Sophie stood there for a moment, staring at the door, her heart hammering in her chest. The weight of Daniel's warning, his betrayal, hung over her like a storm cloud. What had just happened? What was going on between her, Alexander, and the rest of the household? Was Daniel right? Was she really in over her head?

The knock came again, more insistent this time. Sophie took a deep breath and opened the door. Mrs. Laurent stood there, her expression as stern as ever.

"It's time, Miss Carter," she said, her eyes flicking over Sophie with a disapproving glance.

Sophie nodded, forcing a smile she didn't feel. "Right. I'll be there in a moment."

As she walked past Mrs. Laurent and down the hall, her mind kept drifting back to Daniel's words, to the dark truth he had shared with her. Was Alexander really as dangerous as he seemed? And if so, what did that mean for Emma? For her?

Her heart raced as she approached the study where Emma was waiting, and she knew, deep down, that everything was about to change. The walls were closing in, and no matter how hard she tried to stay focused on Emma, she couldn't ignore the growing suspicion in her chest.

She was playing a game she didn't understand. And if she wasn't careful, it could cost her more than she realized.

Nine

A Public Scandal

The morning light crept through the heavy curtains of Sophie's room, casting faint beams of sunlight across the floor. The soft golden glow should have felt peaceful, but it only added to the weight pressing against her chest. Her mind was a hurricane of thoughts—about Alexander, about Emma, about what she had learned from Daniel's warning. The world felt as though it was closing in on her, and no matter how hard she tried to focus on her work, every moment seemed to draw her further into something she didn't fully understand.

She hadn't seen Alexander since the conversation the night before. Not a word had passed between them, and though the mansion was large, it was impossible to ignore the quiet tension in the air. There was a stillness that seemed to hang around her like a thick fog, and every room felt colder than the last.

Sophie stared out of the window, her mind wandering back to the words Daniel had spoken. "You think you can change him?" he had asked, mocking her. "You can't fix what's broken inside him."

But was that what she had been trying to do? Fix him? No. She wasn't trying to change Alexander. She was trying to understand him, to help him understand that there was more to life than control and fear. But now, after hearing Daniel's warning, Sophie wasn't sure anymore. She didn't know what her role was here—what kind of game she was playing. The more she tried to help, the more it seemed like the stakes were rising.

A soft knock on the door interrupted her thoughts. Sophie turned, feeling a rush of nerves. Was it Daniel again, or someone else? She didn't know if she was ready to face any more difficult conversations today.

When she opened the door, it was Emma standing there, looking up at her with those big blue-gray eyes that always seemed to carry a weight beyond her years.

"Morning, Miss Carter," Emma said softly, her voice carefully neutral.

Sophie smiled, trying to shake off the tension from the past few days. "Good morning, Emma. How did you sleep?"

Emma didn't answer right away, instead glancing over her shoulder as though checking for someone. The sudden gesture made Sophie pause. What was going on?

"I slept okay," Emma said, her gaze still distant, her posture stiff as always. "I wanted to talk to you."

Sophie stepped aside to let Emma in, trying to push the uneasy feeling gnawing at her stomach aside. "Of course. What's on your mind?"

Emma walked to the small armchair by the window, her small hands gripping the back of it as if she were holding herself together. Sophie's heart ached at the sight. Emma had always been so controlled, so careful, but now there was something more fragile in her demeanor. Something Sophie hadn't seen before.

"I heard things last night," Emma said quietly, not looking at Sophie. "Things about my father."

Sophie's pulse quickened. She tried to keep her voice calm, steady. "What kind of things?"

Emma hesitated, then spoke in a low voice. "I heard him yelling. Not at me, but at someone else. I didn't see who. But it sounded bad."

Sophie swallowed, trying to keep her emotions in check. Alexander yelling—she had never seen that side of him. But then again, Sophie didn't really know him, did she? She had only seen the façade he presented, the cold, calculated exterior.

"I didn't mean to eavesdrop," Emma added quickly, her voice shaking slightly. "I was just in the hallway, and I heard him. He sounded… angry. But not just angry—like he was… broken. Do you know what I mean?"

Sophie didn't answer right away. She simply nodded. Emma wasn't the only one who had felt it. That strange, magnetic tension between herself and Alexander, that crack in his armor—Sophie had felt it too. And the more she thought about it, the more she realized that whatever was going on with Alexander, it wasn't just about his daughter. It was about him.

"I'm sorry, Emma," Sophie finally said, her voice soft. "I don't know exactly what happened last night, but if you ever need to talk, I'm here for you."

Emma looked up, her eyes searching Sophie's face. Then, after a long pause, she nodded.

"Thanks, Miss Carter," Emma said quietly. "I think I'm okay. But I don't think he'll ever let anyone get close to him. Not for real."

Sophie felt the sting of Emma's words. Emma's father was a man who had built walls so high that even his own daughter felt the distance.

"Maybe… maybe it's better if we don't try to get too close,"

Emma said, almost to herself. "Then no one gets hurt."

Sophie's heart sank. She wanted to argue, to tell Emma that she deserved better than this cold, detached existence. But how could she? She had barely scratched the surface of understanding what was really going on in this house. And now, after hearing Emma's words, Sophie felt more confused than ever.

Before Sophie could say anything else, a sudden loud ringing cut through the silence. It was Sophie's phone. She glanced at the screen, her stomach dropping as soon as she saw the name.

It was the agency that had placed her here.

"Excuse me for a moment," Sophie said, her voice tight. "I need to take this."

Emma nodded and turned to leave the room, but Sophie caught a glimpse of something in her eyes—a flicker of fear, of something unspoken. Emma was hiding more than she let on, but Sophie didn't know how to help her.

Sophie answered the phone, her hands trembling slightly. "Hello?"

"Sophie," the voice on the other end was familiar, but there was a sharp edge to it. "We need to talk."

Sophie's stomach twisted. "What's wrong?" she asked, her voice shaking now.

"I'm afraid there's a problem," the agent said. "There's a story breaking about the Wolfe family. Something involving the household and—" The voice hesitated. "I'm not sure how to say this, but your name has come up."

Sophie's heart skipped. "My name? What do you mean?"

"I don't have all the details yet, but there's a leak. A photo of you and Mr. Wolfe—" the agent said, "—has been released to the press."

Sophie's blood ran cold. "What? How? What kind of photo?"

The agent sighed. "It looks like you were seen in the garden. Talking. A lot more closely than what's considered appropriate for a nanny. The media's picked up on it. There's talk of a relationship between you and Alexander Wolfe."

Sophie's mind raced. She had never been alone with Alexander like that—never crossed any lines. But the photo, she could only imagine how it looked. She had been standing close to him, probably too close, but it wasn't what the press would see. They wouldn't see the hours of tense silence, the hard truths they'd spoken, the walls she had tried to break down. No, they'd see what they wanted to see—scandal.

The phone call felt like it was suffocating her. "I—I don't know how that happened. There's no story here."

But the agent's voice was colder now. "It doesn't matter. The story's already out there. You're being asked to step down immediately. The Wolfe family is demanding it."

Sophie's stomach lurched. She felt like the world was spinning out of control. "But I haven't done anything wrong!"

"It doesn't matter," the agent replied, the finality in their tone making Sophie's blood run cold. "The Wolfe family is a business. And they won't tolerate scandal, even if it's unfounded."

Sophie closed her eyes, her heart pounding in her chest. She had been caught in a game she didn't even know she was playing, and now it was all crashing down. Everything she had worked for, everything she had hoped to achieve here, was slipping away.

Sophie's thoughts spun in a frantic whirl. She couldn't leave—not yet. She couldn't just walk away from Emma, from everything she had come to care about. But staying could mean more than just a lost job—it could mean a public scandal that could ruin her reputation forever.

The moment the phone call ended, Sophie stood frozen in the middle of the room, the weight of everything crashing down on her. She could feel the world shifting, the walls closing in around her. She had no idea what to do, where to go. And somewhere, in the back of her mind, she couldn't shake the feeling that Alexander knew this would happen.

Had he been watching her all along? Had he orchestrated this entire situation?

Sophie shook her head, trying to clear the fog of confusion that had settled over her. One thing was certain. The game had changed. And now, she wasn't just fighting for Emma's future—she was fighting for her own survival.

Ten

The Masquerade Gala

Sophie had barely slept the night before, the weight of the scandal looming over her. She couldn't shake the feeling that something was wrong, that she was being pulled deeper into a game she didn't fully understand. The image of Alexander's face—the way he had looked at her that night—had stayed with her, haunting her thoughts. He was powerful, relentless, a man who controlled everything in his life. And yet, beneath that veneer, Sophie had caught glimpses of something fragile—something that made her question his motives, his intentions, and her own place in his world.

The phone call from the agency had left her shaken, and the media frenzy that followed had been both overwhelming and humiliating. The story was everywhere—headlines in every paper, gossip sites covering every angle. The photo of her and Alexander in the garden had been twisted into something it wasn't. To the public, it looked like an affair, a forbidden romance. But it was nothing like that.

She had tried to ignore the whispers, the stares, the texts from old friends asking if she was okay. But nothing prepared her for what was to come next. She had been summoned to the Wolfe estate that evening, invited to a charity gala held in Alexander's honor. The invitation, in its simplicity, seemed far from ordinary. It was a lavish event, with the elite of the business world in attendance, and Sophie had been instructed to attend in a role she had not expected. She wasn't just the nanny anymore. She was a guest of honor.

The thought unsettled her.

Everything about tonight felt like a test, and Sophie wasn't sure if she was ready for whatever game Alexander had in mind. Was it an olive branch? A way for him to prove his control over her? Or was it something else entirely?

Sophie had spent the better part of the day preparing for the gala, choosing a simple yet elegant black dress that fell just below her knees. The dress was fitted, but not too tight—classy, understated. She applied makeup carefully, doing her best to look confident, even though the weight of everything pressing on her shoulders felt unbearable. Her hair was pulled back in a low bun, and she stood in front of the mirror for a long moment, trying to find a version of herself that she could face tonight.

But when she arrived at the mansion, the atmosphere was

The Masquerade Gala

nothing like what she had expected. The grand entryway was filled with people—dressed to the nines, gliding past her in elegant gowns and sharply tailored suits. But there was no warmth, no genuine human connection. The people milling about were cold, calculating, eyes locked on the event in front of them—power, money, status. That was all they saw. That was all they cared about.

Sophie felt like an outsider, a fish out of water, suddenly aware of how different she was from the people around her. They all belonged to a world she had never been a part of. The whispers, the sidelong glances—she could feel them as she walked through the crowd, but she held her head high, unwilling to let them see the storm churning inside her.

As she stepped into the ballroom, the opulence of the space took her breath away. Crystal chandeliers hung from the high ceiling, casting a soft glow over the polished marble floors. The walls were lined with priceless artwork, and the grand piano in the corner was being played by a musician in a black tuxedo. Guests mingled in small groups, drinks in hand, their laughter echoing off the walls.

Sophie scanned the room, her heart racing. Where was Alexander? She had been told to wait for him before doing anything, but she had no idea what that meant. Was he watching her? Or was he simply going to leave her to navigate this strange world alone?

The sound of heels clicking against the floor drew her attention. She turned just as Mrs. Laurent approached, her expression unreadable, her eyes sweeping over Sophie as if she were a mere intruder.

"Miss Carter," Mrs. Laurent said, her voice sharp as always. "I see you've made yourself presentable. Mr. Wolfe will be with you shortly."

"Thank you," Sophie replied, her voice calm despite the nerves twisting in her stomach. She was here for Emma. She had to remember that. No matter how strange or uncomfortable this event felt, her priority was still the girl she had promised to protect.

Mrs. Laurent gave a terse nod, then walked away without another word. Sophie exhaled slowly, feeling the weight of her role pressing down on her. She had no idea what Alexander's plans were, but she knew he had orchestrated this evening for a reason.

Minutes later, the doors to the ballroom opened, and Alexander stepped into the room, his presence commanding the attention of everyone around him. He was wearing a tailored tuxedo, his broad shoulders filling the space with an almost tangible magnetism. The way he carried himself—so confident, so at ease in this world—made Sophie feel out of place, like an imposter in the midst of a grand performance.

And yet, when his eyes met hers across the room, something in Sophie's chest fluttered. His gaze softened for a brief moment, a flicker of something more vulnerable crossing his features, before he turned away, his attention quickly shifting back to

The Masquerade Gala

the crowd. The mask was back in place. The moment was gone.

The night stretched on, and Sophie found herself caught in the whirl of it all. She was introduced to a handful of people—high-profile businessmen and women, investors, dignitaries—all of them sizing her up, smiling politely but with the undercurrent of calculation. Sophie felt like a piece of furniture at a dinner party. No one truly saw her, not as a person, but as a symbol. She was a part of the image Alexander wanted to project, a footnote in a grand performance.

And then, unexpectedly, Alexander approached her.

Sophie's pulse quickened as he stopped in front of her, his sharp gaze taking in her every movement. He was holding a glass of champagne, but his attention was entirely focused on her.

"You look stunning tonight, Miss Carter," he said, his voice smooth, almost too smooth. But there was an edge to it, a dangerous undertone that sent a shiver down her spine. His gaze lingered on her for a beat longer than necessary, and Sophie forced herself not to look away.

"Thank you," she said, trying to keep her voice steady. "You look… well, as expected."

He smirked slightly, his lips curling into something almost imperceptible. "You always have such a way with words."

Sophie didn't respond to the comment. Instead, she studied

him. She had seen him at his most vulnerable—had seen the man who was just a father, struggling with his own grief and fear. But here, in this setting, he was a different version of himself. He was the businessman, the patriarch, the man who ruled this world with an iron fist. And the distance between them felt more real than ever.

"Enjoying the party?" he asked, his tone casual, though Sophie could hear the undertone of command in his voice.

"It's… quite overwhelming," she replied honestly. "But I suppose that's to be expected."

"Don't worry," he said, his eyes scanning the room for a moment. "You'll get used to it."

But Sophie couldn't shake the feeling that there was more to this than just an invitation to a party. It was as though Alexander had planned this evening to make a statement. But what was it? Was it a chance to keep up appearances, to prove something to the outside world? Or was it a test of some kind—a way for him to measure her loyalty, her resolve?

Before she could voice her thoughts, the sound of laughter broke through the air. A man in a sharply tailored suit approached them—another figure of importance in Alexander's world. His name, Sophie knew, was Jonathan Hargrave—a high-ranking investor, one of Alexander's closest allies. He greeted Alexander warmly, shaking his hand before turning his attention to Sophie.

The Masquerade Gala

"Ah, Miss Carter, so lovely to see you here tonight," Jonathan said with a wide smile. His eyes swept over her appraisingly, and Sophie felt the hairs on the back of her neck rise.

Before she could respond, another voice interrupted them.

"Isn't it just lovely to have the whole family together?"

Sophie turned quickly, her stomach dropping when she saw Emma, dressed in a delicate white dress, walking toward them. Her eyes were wide and cautious, and though she smiled, there was something hollow about it, as though she had been carefully trained to act this way. Sophie's heart ached for her.

Alexander's face softened just slightly at the sight of his daughter, but the moment passed quickly.

"Emma, darling," he said, stepping forward to greet her. "You look beautiful tonight."

Emma nodded quietly, her eyes flicking over to Sophie for just a second before she turned away. "Thank you, Father."

Sophie's chest tightened. The girl was a child, but she was already so carefully controlled, so aware of the masks she was forced to wear. Sophie wanted to reach out to her, to tell her it was okay to be a child, to let go of the facade, but she knew that would only expose Emma to more danger.

"Join us," Alexander said to Emma, gesturing for her to stay by his side. "We're in the middle of an interesting conversation."

The Nanny's Billionaire Boss exposed

As Emma took her place beside him, Sophie felt the weight of the moment settle over her like a thick fog. She was part of this world now—whether she wanted to be or not. And the longer she stayed in it, the more she realized that Alexander Wolfe wasn't just a man trying to protect his daughter. He was someone who would stop at nothing to keep control, even if it meant destroying everything around him.

The masquerade was just beginning. And Sophie knew she was already in too deep.

Eleven

Betrayal and Fury

The gala had been in full swing for nearly two hours by the time Sophie felt the walls closing in. The champagne had been flowing, the music swelling, the guests laughing and exchanging pleasantries as though everything was perfectly in order. But behind the façade, Sophie could feel the tension building, thickening in the air like an impending storm. Every glance, every smile felt calculated, and every word she spoke seemed to be scrutinized. She couldn't escape the feeling that she was nothing more than a pawn in a game she didn't understand.

She had stayed by Alexander's side as the evening wore on, playing her part in this grand charade. He had introduced her to more important figures—each one colder than the last, each one viewing her through the lens of suspicion, as though she were somehow beneath them. It was clear that she wasn't just a nanny to them; she was a liability, a mystery to be probed.

But through it all, Sophie had kept her composure, smiling when she was expected to, nodding in approval when necessary. She kept her distance from Alexander, though, allowing the space between them to grow. His gaze hadn't softened much since the first time their eyes had locked across the ballroom. And yet, despite the distance, Sophie felt his presence in a way that made it almost impossible to breathe. His cold, calculating demeanor had returned, and he seemed to view her as nothing more than another part of his public image. The vulnerable, broken man she had glimpsed in their private conversation the night before seemed to have disappeared entirely.

Sophie wasn't sure what she had expected from the evening, but it certainly wasn't this. It wasn't the carefully orchestrated performance of wealth and power, nor the chilling indifference Alexander had shown toward her since they'd arrived. She had hoped that, maybe, just maybe, there was a chance to break through the walls he had built around himself. But now, it felt like she had been used—pulled into this world to fulfill a role that wasn't hers to play.

She couldn't shake the sensation that something darker was lurking beneath the surface. There was something Alexander wasn't telling her, something important. And as much as she wanted to focus on Emma and her well-being, she couldn't ignore the gnawing suspicion that the truth about this family—and about Alexander—was far more complicated than she had ever imagined.

Betrayal and Fury

Her thoughts were interrupted by the sound of a voice behind her.

"Sophie, there you are."

She turned to find Daniel, looking as composed and cold as ever, his eyes scanning the crowd with a sharpness that almost made her uncomfortable. He was dressed in a perfectly tailored tuxedo, his posture rigid, his expression unreadable. Despite the grandeur of the event, there was an unmistakable tension around him—a quiet danger.

"I didn't expect to see you here," he said, his lips curling into something like a smile, but it never quite reached his eyes.

Sophie forced a smile of her own, though she didn't feel it. "I didn't expect to be here either," she replied, her voice laced with more bitterness than she intended.

Daniel's gaze flickered over her, his eyes narrowing as if he could sense the unease roiling beneath her composed exterior. "You look... beautiful tonight," he said, the words almost mechanical, as though he were saying them because it was expected, not because he actually meant them.

"Thank you," Sophie said stiffly. She didn't know why, but her instinct was to step back, to put distance between herself and him. She had been careful to keep her interactions with Daniel as professional as possible since their heated conversation in her room, but tonight... tonight everything felt more dangerous. She wasn't sure if it was just the tension in the air, or if Daniel himself was the source of that feeling.

"Can I get you a drink?" he asked, his tone suddenly shifting. He looked around, as if searching for a way to keep her occupied, or perhaps to distract her from something. "A quiet place to talk, perhaps?"

Sophie frowned, her instincts flaring. There was something about his offer that didn't sit right with her. "I'm fine," she said quickly, her voice firm. She didn't need more of his cryptic words. She didn't need to be pulled into whatever game he was playing.

Daniel's lips tightened, the flicker of a challenge in his eyes. But he didn't press further. Instead, he stepped back, his gaze lingering on her for a moment longer than necessary. "Very well," he said, his voice clipped. "But be careful, Sophie. Not everything is as it seems here."

The words hung in the air like a warning, but before Sophie could respond, Daniel had already turned and walked away, melting into the crowd of guests who were far too busy enjoying themselves to notice the tension between them.

Sophie's heart was pounding now, her mind racing. Not everything was as it seemed? What did Daniel know that she didn't? And why did she feel like she was being watched?

The thought was chilling. She glanced around the ballroom, her eyes scanning the guests, looking for any sign of someone who might be watching her too closely. But everyone appeared to be absorbed in their own conversations, their laughter echoing off the marble walls.

Then, a cold gust of air washed over her, and Sophie turned sharply, instinctively stepping back. But it wasn't the chill in the room that made her pulse quicken. It was him—Alexander—standing at the far side of the room, his piercing gaze locked on her.

For a moment, their eyes met, and Sophie felt the weight of his stare like a physical force. The world around her seemed to fade away, and for the briefest of moments, it felt as though they were the only two people in the room. He was studying her, as though trying to read her every thought, every feeling. She didn't know how he did it, but it was as if he could see right through her.

A flicker of something—recognition?—passed between them, but before Sophie could process it, Alexander's gaze shifted. He turned away, making his way toward the large staircase at the back of the room.

Sophie's breath caught in her throat. She didn't know why, but she felt an undeniable pull toward him. She knew she shouldn't follow him, shouldn't get any closer. But something inside her urged her to move. Her body reacted before her mind could catch up.

She made her way across the ballroom, slipping between guests and moving toward the staircase, trying to ignore the feeling of being drawn toward him.

As she reached the foot of the stairs, she found Alexander standing there, his back turned to her, his posture relaxed but still commanding. He didn't look surprised to see her.

"You don't belong here," he said, his voice low, almost a whisper, as he turned to face her. There was a flicker of something—something Sophie couldn't quite place—behind his eyes.

Sophie swallowed, her heart hammering in her chest. "What do you mean?" she asked, her voice barely audible.

"You've already crossed a line," he said, his words deliberate, each one cutting through the air like a sharp blade. "You've already made your choice."

Sophie felt a chill run through her. "What choice?" she asked, her voice shaking despite her best efforts to remain calm.

Alexander's gaze softened, just slightly, but it was enough to make Sophie's heart beat faster. "The choice to be here. To stay close to me." He paused, the tension between them palpable. "I don't allow attachments, Sophie. Not anymore."

The words hit Sophie like a punch to the gut. He was trying to push her away—he was trying to make her understand that she was just another pawn, just another piece of the game.

But Sophie wasn't going to back down.

"Maybe you don't get to decide that for me," she said, her voice stronger now, though her heart was still pounding in her chest.

Betrayal and Fury

For a long moment, Alexander didn't speak. Instead, he looked at her, his expression unreadable. Then, finally, he nodded. "Maybe not."

And just as quickly, he turned and walked away, leaving Sophie standing at the base of the stairs, feeling more alone than ever before.

Twelve

The Masquerade Unmasked

Sophie couldn't shake the feeling that she was drowning in the chaos of the night. The masquerade gala had turned into a tangled mess of half-truths and deception, and despite her best efforts to stay composed, every moment seemed to pull her deeper into a storm she wasn't prepared for.

The brief exchange with Alexander had left her shaken. There had been something final about his words, something that made her question everything she thought she understood. He didn't want her close. He didn't want attachments. Yet the way he had looked at her earlier—how he had studied her, as if trying to peel away her layers—told a different story. Sophie had crossed a line, he said. But the truth was, she hadn't crossed a line—he had built the line, and she had simply stepped over it. And now, it felt like the weight of his walls was closing in on her.

The Masquerade Unmasked

She stood alone at the edge of the ballroom, trying to collect herself amidst the haze of music, laughter, and clinking glasses. The glass of champagne in her hand felt heavy, too heavy for her, but she didn't dare set it down. It was the only thing anchoring her to the present moment, to a world that felt increasingly alien.

The guests around her moved in waves—empty, false smiles exchanged between well-dressed people whose conversations didn't touch anything real. Sophie felt like an outsider, a ghost in a room full of masks. She wasn't meant to be here. She wasn't meant to play this part in Alexander's world. But somewhere, deep in her gut, she knew that she had been drawn into this world for a reason.

Her thoughts were interrupted by the soft sound of footsteps approaching her. She turned sharply, instinctively tightening her grip on her glass, expecting to see Daniel, or even Mrs. Laurent, walking toward her with some carefully rehearsed words. But it was neither of them. It was Emma.

The young girl's face was a picture of detachment, her eyes wide and watchful, as though she had learned how to wear her emotions like armor. She was still in her white dress, her hair meticulously styled. She didn't belong here, Sophie thought. She was too young, too innocent, for this world of polished smiles and hidden agendas. And yet, Emma had already been shaped by it—trained to live in the shadows of her father's empire.

Sophie gave her a small, uncertain smile. "Emma. Is everything okay?"

Emma nodded slowly, but her gaze flickered nervously to the crowd, her lips pressed tightly together. "Father wanted me to stay out of the way," she said quietly. "He doesn't want me to get in the way of the important people."

Sophie's heart twisted. Emma's words felt like they were soaked in a lifetime of conditioning, a quiet surrender to the expectations of the world around her. It wasn't the first time Sophie had heard this kind of sentiment from Emma. The girl was already so aware of her place, of her role to be seen but never truly heard.

"I'm sorry, Emma," Sophie said gently. "You don't have to stay out of the way. You belong here too, you know?"

Emma looked at her, and for the first time that evening, Sophie saw a flicker of something other than stoic control in the girl's eyes—something that looked like longing, like she wanted to believe Sophie's words but couldn't.

"Thank you," Emma said, though there was little conviction in her voice. She paused, biting her lip as though unsure of whether or not to say more. Then, before Sophie could ask, Emma turned abruptly, her small figure weaving through the crowd as she moved away from Sophie.

Sophie watched her go, feeling a pang of helplessness in her chest. Emma was still just a child, but she had already learned how to hide herself, to shrink beneath the weight of this life. Sophie knew she couldn't fix everything for her, but she couldn't let Emma fade into the background. Not again.

Before she could follow Emma, a movement caught her eye—a familiar, too-familiar movement. Alexander. He was across the room, standing near the grand staircase, his back to her as he spoke with a man Sophie didn't recognize. The man was tall, broad-shouldered, and dressed in a sharp suit. From the way Alexander interacted with him, Sophie could tell the man wasn't just an acquaintance; there was a deeper connection, a bond that went beyond simple business.

Sophie's heart rate quickened. She hadn't expected him to come to her after their brief conversation earlier. She wasn't sure what she had expected, but it wasn't this—this cold detachment. The ice that surrounded Alexander had returned, and it chilled her to the bone.

The man who stood with him laughed at something Alexander said, his voice boisterous, but Alexander didn't laugh. He didn't smile. He stood there, his hands clasped behind his back, his eyes scanning the room as if searching for something—or someone.

Sophie's stomach dropped as the man turned slightly, revealing his face. Jonathan Hargrave.

The name clicked into place. He was one of the biggest investors in Alexander's companies, a man known for his ruthless business tactics and his insatiable thirst for power. Sophie had heard rumors about him, rumors that painted him as a man who would do anything to win—even at the expense of his moral compass.

She had no doubt that the conversation between the two men was one of business, one of strategy, but the unease creeping up her spine told her there was something more. There was something in the way they looked at each other, the way their words seemed to carry an edge. Sophie didn't like it.

The more she watched them, the more she realized how dangerous the people in this room really were. This wasn't just a gala. This wasn't just a charity event.

This was a battlefield. A battlefield for power, for control. And Sophie was caught in the middle of it all, with no way out.

Just as Sophie turned to retreat into the shadows, she felt a familiar presence beside her. It was Daniel.

His dark eyes locked onto her with a cold intensity. He didn't greet her, didn't say anything to acknowledge her presence. He just stared at her for a moment, his gaze piercing. Sophie could feel the weight of his scrutiny, and it made her stomach churn.

"You're still here," he said, his voice low and deliberate, like each word had weight.

Sophie tried to maintain her composure, but the flicker of fear in her chest was hard to ignore. "Of course I'm still here," she replied, her voice sharp, almost defiant. "What do you want, Daniel?"

He didn't respond right away. Instead, he studied her as if weighing her every move. His lips barely curled into a smile, but it wasn't the friendly kind. It was a taunting smile, one that suggested he knew more than he was willing to share.

"You've made quite the impression tonight," he said slowly, his voice low and cutting. "Alexander won't like it if you keep drawing attention to yourself. Especially not after the… scandal."

Sophie's breath caught in her throat. "I haven't done anything wrong," she said, her voice steady despite the growing unease.

Daniel chuckled darkly. "The problem is, Sophie, that you're not in control here. And the more you push against it, the more you'll find yourself trapped."

The words hung in the air between them, thick with the weight of their implications. Sophie's heart raced. She knew he wasn't just talking about the evening—he was talking about her entire role in this house. About Emma. About Alexander.

"You think you have power here," Daniel continued, his voice almost a whisper now. "But you're just another piece on his chessboard."

Sophie felt her pulse quicken. She didn't know what kind of game Daniel was playing, but she didn't like it. She didn't like the way he was looking at her, the way his words made her feel smaller, weaker, like she was caught in the web of a trap she couldn't see.

"I'm not a piece, Daniel," she said, her voice shaky but defiant. "I'm not a pawn. I won't be anyone's pawn."

For a moment, Daniel just looked at her, his expression unreadable. Then, without another word, he turned and walked away, disappearing into the crowd of guests.

Sophie stood there, her breath shallow, the weight of his words still hanging over her like a cloud. The room seemed to spin around her, the laughter and clinking glasses blurring into the background as she tried to make sense of everything.

She had crossed a line. She had gotten too close. And now, it seemed, there was no way out.

The game had already begun, and Sophie had no idea how it was going to end.

Thirteen

A Dangerous Game

Sophie felt the weight of the evening pressing down on her like a vice, each moment more suffocating than the last. The masquerade gala had long since passed the point of being a simple social event. What had started as a carefully crafted façade of elegance and grace had transformed into something far darker. She could feel it—the tension in the air, thick with unspoken threats, and the cold calculation in every smile exchanged. Sophie had tried to play her part, to blend in, but now she knew that nothing about this evening was normal.

She had barely managed to escape the suffocating whispers and probing glances of the other guests, retreating into a quiet corner of the ballroom where the shadows seemed to offer some form of solace. But there was no real escape. Not tonight. Not in this house.

The crystal chandeliers above cast long shadows across the room, their flickering light adding to the haunting atmosphere. The elegant décor, the distant music, the soft murmur of voices—it all felt like a nightmare she couldn't wake up from. Sophie's chest tightened with every passing second, the unease crawling under her skin. There was no one she could trust here. Not Daniel, not Mrs. Laurent, not even Alexander.

She had caught a glimpse of him earlier, speaking with Jonathan Hargrave, the man she had seen earlier in the evening. The conversation had been hushed, too private for anyone to overhear. But Sophie had felt the energy shift, the subtle intensity between them that only confirmed what she already feared: whatever game Alexander was playing, it was one she hadn't been prepared for.

A soft sound behind her made Sophie stiffen. She didn't need to turn around to know who it was. The air grew heavier the moment he entered her space, the magnetic pull of his presence undeniable. Alexander.

She felt his gaze before she saw him, the weight of it pressing down on her back like a physical force. Her heart pounded in her chest as the distance between them closed. She hadn't expected him to come looking for her after their brief exchange earlier. But here he was, stepping into the corner where she had hidden herself, his eyes dark and unreadable.

"I didn't expect to find you here," he said, his voice low, a slight edge to his tone. It wasn't a question. It was a statement.

Sophie straightened, her spine stiffening in the face of his nearness. She didn't want to give him the satisfaction of knowing how much his presence affected her. "I needed some air," she said, her voice steady, though she could feel the tension building in her stomach. "This night is a bit… overwhelming."

Alexander's eyes flickered over her, as though measuring her every word, every movement. There was something about the way he looked at her—something that felt like a challenge. "I've noticed you've been keeping your distance," he said, his gaze lingering a fraction too long. "I'm starting to think you're avoiding me."

Sophie forced herself to meet his gaze, but inside, her mind was whirling. She couldn't afford to let him control the conversation, not tonight. "I'm not avoiding you," she said, her voice colder than she intended. "I'm just trying to make sense of everything. Trying to understand what exactly I'm doing here."

The corner of Alexander's mouth curled into a small, almost imperceptible smile. "You're here because I asked you to be," he replied. His voice was calm, but there was something in his words that made Sophie's pulse quicken.

She crossed her arms over her chest, her breath coming in shallow bursts. "And what exactly do you expect from me?" she asked, her voice thick with suspicion. "You've kept me at arm's length this entire time. So why bring me here tonight?"

He stepped closer, his presence filling the small space between them, and Sophie had to fight the urge to take a step back. He was so close, too close for comfort. "I'm not keeping you at arm's length, Sophie," he said, his voice dropping lower. "I'm simply letting you see the truth. The truth about this family. The truth about who I am."

Sophie could feel the heat radiating off him, could feel the intensity in his gaze. It was suffocating, overwhelming, and yet she couldn't look away. "And what's the truth, Alexander?" she whispered, her voice suddenly fragile. "What is it you want from me?"

His expression softened just a fraction, though the coldness never fully disappeared. "I want you to understand that this is not a game. It's never been a game." His eyes darkened, and Sophie felt her stomach tighten. "You're here because I need you to see things for what they are. Because, in the end, this is the only way I know how to protect what matters."

Sophie's heart skipped a beat. She couldn't tell if he was being honest or if this was just another part of his carefully constructed facade. But she knew, deep down, that something in his words resonated with her—something dark, something dangerous that she hadn't fully understood until now.

"You don't need to protect me, Alexander," she said softly, her voice trembling with the weight of the moment. "I don't want to be part of this... this world."

For a moment, there was silence. A long silence, stretching between them, thick with everything they hadn't said. Sophie could feel the heaviness in the air, the tension so palpable that it was almost suffocating. Then, without warning, Alexander stepped back, as if a part of him had pulled away. The coldness returned to his eyes, but there was something new in the way he looked at her—something sharper, something that made her heart race even faster.

"I don't expect you to understand," he said, his voice clipped. "But you will. You'll understand why everything is this way, why I have to keep control."

Sophie swallowed hard. "Control? Is that all this is to you? Is everything just about control?"

Alexander looked at her, his expression unreadable, but there was a flicker of something—something she couldn't quite place—beneath the surface. "In this world, Sophie, control is the only thing that matters. You don't survive without it."

The words hit her like a physical blow. Sophie had never fully realized how far gone Alexander was, how deeply entrenched in this world of power and manipulation he had become. She had thought she could reach him, that somehow, he was still the man who had opened up to her in the quiet moments of vulnerability. But now, standing before him, she felt the full force of his calculation.

She wanted to say more, wanted to push him, to demand the truth, but something stopped her. Something told her that if she kept pushing, if she kept trying to tear away the layers of his carefully crafted exterior, there was a price to pay. A price that might cost her more than just her job. It might cost her something far more important.

Sophie opened her mouth to speak, but before she could, a sudden noise shattered the tension in the room. The sound of a glass breaking, followed by a gasp.

They both turned toward the source of the disturbance. Across the ballroom, Emma stood frozen, her face pale, her hands trembling as she looked down at the shattered glass at her feet. Guests were crowding around her, but none of them seemed to know what to do. Sophie's heart leaped into her throat as she saw the look on Emma's face—a mixture of shock and fear, a look that Sophie had seen all too often in her eyes.

Without thinking, Sophie rushed across the room, ignoring the murmurs from the guests and the uncomfortable glances thrown her way. She reached Emma just as the girl's knees buckled beneath her, her face pale and stricken with panic.

"Emma!" Sophie called, kneeling beside her.

But Emma didn't look at her. Her eyes were fixed on the crowd, her body shaking as if she had been caught in some unseen trap. Sophie reached out, placing a hand gently on her arm, but Emma flinched away, her eyes wide with terror.

"Emma, what happened?" Sophie asked softly, her voice trembling. "It's okay. You're safe."

But Emma didn't respond. Instead, her voice broke, barely a

whisper. "I… I didn't mean to… I didn't mean to…"

Sophie's heart ached. She pulled Emma into her arms, trying to calm her, but Emma wasn't listening. She was somewhere far away, trapped in her own fear, trapped in the shadows of this life.

And Sophie realized, with growing dread, that she wasn't just dealing with a child in need of protection. She was dealing with a family who had already broken. A family where love and trust had been shattered long ago, and now, all that was left was a game that no one could win.

And no matter how hard Sophie tried to play by the rules, she knew she was already in too deep. The stakes had never been higher.

Fourteen

The Unraveling

The moment Emma trembled in Sophie's arms, everything seemed to fall apart. Sophie had expected the night to be filled with political conversations and empty pleasantries, but now, as Emma clung to her, it was clear that the underbelly of the Wolfe family was far darker than she had imagined. Emma's panic was like a small spark that ignited a deep-seated fear in Sophie—fear for the girl, but also for herself.

Sophie held Emma close, trying to steady the child's rapid breaths, her heart pounding as the crowd murmured around them. She didn't know what had happened, only that something had triggered Emma—something deep inside her that Sophie couldn't yet understand.

"Shh, it's okay," Sophie whispered, her voice as soothing as she could make it. She rubbed Emma's back gently, hoping to calm her. But the girl wasn't responding, her eyes distant and unfocused, lost in some internal struggle. Sophie glanced up toward the growing group of onlookers. The whispered rumors had already begun.

"Move away," someone said coldly, and Sophie's eyes flickered toward the source of the voice—a tall, sharp-featured man with a sleek black tie, his arms crossed and his face hard as stone.

It was Jonathan Hargrave, and Sophie could already feel the weight of his gaze—sharp, calculating, judging. He had no interest in the well-being of Emma. To him, this was just another inconvenience, a problem that had to be contained.

The crowd shifted uncomfortably, the tension palpable, and Sophie's chest tightened. She had to get Emma out of here. She couldn't allow this to escalate any further, especially not with so many powerful figures watching.

Gently, she lifted Emma from the floor, feeling the fragile weight of the girl in her arms. Emma didn't resist, but her face was pale, her lips trembling as if she were trapped in a nightmare.

"Come on, Emma," Sophie murmured softly, trying to keep her voice steady as she moved through the crowd, the guests stepping aside like they were afraid to get too close. The whispers followed them as Sophie navigated the sea of uncomfortable glances.

But then, a hand grabbed her arm, pulling her back with a force that almost made her lose her balance. Sophie's heart skipped as she turned to find Alexander standing there, his grip firm around her wrist.

"You're taking her somewhere?" His voice was calm but tinged with a deep, simmering anger.

Sophie's pulse raced. "She's not well, Alexander. She needs to rest. Please—"

"She needs nothing from you," he cut her off, his eyes flashing with an emotion she couldn't quite place. "Put her down."

Sophie stood frozen, torn between the instinct to protect Emma and the looming presence of Alexander, whose stare was colder than the room itself. She could feel the tension between them crackling, like a current that was about to break. But Emma—Emma needed to be away from this. Sophie's instincts were screaming at her to get the girl out of here, out of this house, out of this nightmare.

"She's my daughter," Alexander's voice lowered, almost dangerously. His grip tightened, not on her wrist, but around the air between them. "I don't need you playing the role of protector. I told you to stay out of my way."

Sophie pulled her wrist out of his grasp with a sharp movement, her breath catching as she stood tall. "You may be her father, Alexander, but that doesn't mean I'm going to watch you break her. I'll never stand aside when she's suffering."

The words hung between them, raw and defiant. Sophie hadn't meant to say them, but it was too late. She had spoken the truth, and the sting of it settled into the silence that followed.

Alexander's eyes darkened, his jaw tightening as his gaze flickered down to Emma, who still hung limply in Sophie's arms, barely conscious. For a moment, the room seemed to hold its breath.

Then, without warning, Alexander stepped back, his expression hardening into something unrecognizable. "Fine," he said, his voice low, dripping with ice. "Take her. But understand this: you don't know what you're dealing with."

Sophie swallowed, the weight of his words pressing down on her like a physical force. She wanted to argue, wanted to push him, to demand that he stop treating Emma like a commodity, but the exhaustion in Emma's face, the desperate fear in her eyes, stopped her. Sophie turned quickly and started to make her way toward the back of the ballroom, but not without a glance toward Alexander, whose cold gaze followed her every move.

She reached the hallway with Emma still in her arms, the sound of her rapid breathing the only thing keeping her grounded. Sophie wasn't sure where she was going, but she needed to get the girl to safety—somewhere. Anywhere. Just away from the eyes of the guests, away from the suffocating walls of this house.

She passed by a few rooms, each one more opulent than the last, but none of them felt safe. She needed to get out of this mansion. She needed to find a place where Emma could breathe, where they both could be free of the constant pressure of expectations.

Her heart pounded as she turned another corner and found herself facing a heavy wooden door, slightly ajar. The library. It was the one room in the house she hadn't yet explored, and somehow, it felt like the one place that could offer her some privacy.

She pushed the door open, feeling the quiet coolness of the room settle over her like a blanket. She closed the door softly behind her, locking it out of instinct. The library was large, lined with towering shelves filled with books, the air thick with the scent of leather and old paper. But despite its beauty, Sophie couldn't shake the feeling that the walls were closing in on her.

She set Emma down carefully on one of the plush chairs in the corner, kneeling beside her, still trying to calm the girl's breathing. She wiped the sweat from Emma's forehead, whispering reassurances, but Emma didn't respond. Her eyes were glassy, her face pale, and the silence between them was more deafening than anything.

Sophie looked down at Emma, feeling completely helpless. This wasn't just a child's breakdown. This was something deeper—something rooted in fear, fear that Sophie couldn't even begin to understand. She could feel the weight of it, like a heavy burden pressing down on both of them. Sophie was no therapist. She was just a woman who had gotten too involved, who had walked too far into a world that wasn't hers to navigate.

The silence between them was shattered by the sound of a faint knock on the door. Sophie's heart leaped in her chest, and she froze.

"Miss Carter?" came a familiar voice. "It's Mrs. Laurent."

Sophie felt a cold rush of dread flood her veins. She hadn't expected anyone to follow her, but then again, she should have known better. In this house, nothing happened without someone watching.

Sophie stood quickly, but she didn't open the door. She couldn't afford to bring anyone into this moment, not now. Not when Emma needed space.

"Leave me alone," Sophie called out sharply, her voice firm but laced with anxiety. "I don't want to speak with anyone right now."

There was a brief silence before Mrs. Laurent spoke again, her tone cold but controlled. "Miss Carter, I suggest you open the door immediately. Mr. Wolfe has ordered me to escort you back to the main hall."

Sophie's stomach turned. She didn't want to deal with Alexander right now—not when Emma was in this state, not when everything had become so tangled. She wanted to yell, to argue, but something inside her told her it was better to remain silent.

He was controlling everything—every decision, every moment, even the smallest action. Sophie was no longer sure what she was supposed to do or how she was supposed to act.

She took a deep breath, pushing aside the fear and uncertainty that weighed on her, and walked toward the door, her hand hovering over the handle. But as she reached for it, Emma's voice, soft and broken, stopped her in her tracks.

"Don't let them take me back," Emma whispered.

Sophie froze, her heart pounding as she turned back to Emma. The girl's eyes were wide, filled with more fear than Sophie had ever seen. There was something in her gaze—a plea. Something that told Sophie that this moment was not just about one broken child. It was about something far larger. Something that she was still trying to piece together.

Sophie leaned down, brushing a strand of hair from Emma's face, her hand trembling. "I won't let them take you anywhere, Emma," she whispered. "I promise."

But even as she spoke the words, Sophie knew deep down that she was already caught in a trap. She had made a promise to herself that she would protect Emma, but how could she protect her when she didn't even understand the forces at play?

The door knocked again, more insistent this time, and Sophie knew that the walls were closing in, and the game was far from over.

Fifteen

The Unseen Threat

Sophie's fingers tightened around the door handle, the cold metal sending a shock through her body. Her heart raced in her chest, the weight of Emma's plea echoing in her mind. "Don't let them take me back." It was a cry for help that Sophie couldn't ignore, even if the consequences were impossible to predict. She knew something wasn't right—something much darker than she could have imagined.

She turned toward Emma, who was still sitting on the chair in the corner, her small hands clenched tightly in her lap, her eyes wide with a fear Sophie had never seen before. **This wasn't just about a broken glass, or a child misbehaving. Emma was terrified.** Sophie could see it in the way her hands trembled, the way her breaths came shallow and ragged, like she was trying to fight off something invisible.

"I won't let them take you anywhere, Emma," Sophie repeated, her voice soft but determined. She didn't know how, but she would keep her promise. **She had to.**

But what was it that Emma was running from? What had happened to her in this house to make her so terrified? The walls felt like they were closing in. Sophie couldn't shake the feeling that they were in a house full of **secrets**, secrets that no one wanted to admit even existed. And the more she tried to peel away the layers, the more dangerous it became.

The knock on the door came again—this time, louder. Mrs. Laurent's voice drifted through, too calm and too collected to be genuine. "Miss Carter, you need to come back to the ballroom. It's not safe for you to stay in here."

Sophie clenched her jaw. Mrs. Laurent didn't care about her safety, she cared about appearances. Sophie could hear the **command** in her tone, and it only made her more determined not to answer. She turned back to Emma, who had curled her knees to her chest, her face drawn tight with fear.

"Emma, listen to me," Sophie said, crouching down in front of her. "I'm not going anywhere. We're going to figure this out together."

But Emma only shook her head, her lips trembling. "You don't understand. It's not just him. **They**—they won't leave us alone. They never will."

Sophie's heart clenched. **They?** Who was Emma talking about? Was it just Alexander she was scared of? Or was there something else lurking in the shadows of this mansion, something more **sinister** than she could even imagine?

Before Sophie could ask, the door to the library opened just a crack, and Sophie instinctively stepped in front of Emma, her body instinctively protective. She didn't want to let anyone else in—not until she knew what was really going on.

Mrs. Laurent's sharp eyes peered around the door. "Miss Carter," she said again, her voice tight with barely contained annoyance, "I'm afraid I must insist. Mr. Wolfe is waiting for you."

Sophie stood her ground. "I don't want to go back, Mrs. Laurent. Not yet. Not until I know what's going on."

A brief silence stretched between them, heavy with tension. Mrs. Laurent's gaze hardened, and Sophie could see the **frustration** simmering beneath the surface. But she didn't back down. The last thing she wanted to do was go back into that ballroom, into that world of smiles and secrets.

"Mr. Wolfe is not someone you should defy," Mrs. Laurent said finally, her words low and sharp. "You're making a grave mistake. You've already made one by taking Emma away from the crowd."

Sophie's pulse spiked at the mention of Alexander. She turned back to Emma, her protective instincts flaring. **What had Alexander done to her?**

"I'm not going anywhere until I know what's going on, Mrs. Laurent," Sophie said, her voice firm. "You can go tell Mr. Wolfe that I'm not leaving this room until I get some answers."

Mrs. Laurent's eyes flashed with something dangerous, and for a brief moment, Sophie thought the woman might step forward, might force her hand. But then, the door to the ballroom slammed shut, the sound vibrating through the walls. The brief moment of tension was over as quickly as it had begun.

Sophie exhaled slowly, her heart racing, but as the seconds passed, she began to sense something different. Something off about the way Mrs. Laurent had spoken. **Grave mistake.** It wasn't just a warning. It was a threat. And Sophie didn't need to be a genius to understand what kind of threat it was.

"Emma, what are they doing to you?" Sophie whispered, her voice shaking. She kneeled beside the girl, trying to calm her as she saw the terror return to Emma's face.

Emma looked at Sophie for a long moment, her expression unreadable. Then, in a voice so low it was almost a whisper, Emma spoke. "You don't know what they'll do. He won't stop. He won't let us be normal."

Sophie's chest constricted. She wanted to ask her, to demand more, but she didn't have time. Her eyes darted toward the door. She could feel the weight of the moment pressing down on her.

She was running out of time.

Before Sophie could say anything more, the sound of heavy footsteps outside the door made her freeze. She glanced back

The Unseen Threat

at Emma, whose eyes were wide with terror.

"Hide," Sophie whispered urgently. "Please. I'll protect you."

But Emma didn't move. She remained perfectly still, staring at Sophie with wide, **haunted eyes**. There was something about her expression, something in the way she held herself, that told Sophie that this was no ordinary moment. There was a deep **pain** in Emma's gaze, something she couldn't fix with kind words or reassurances.

The doorknob turned with a soft click. Sophie's heart leapt in her chest as the door began to creak open, and she quickly stepped in front of Emma, her body blocking the view from anyone who might enter.

The door opened fully, and there, standing in the doorway, was **Alexander**. His presence was overpowering, his eyes cold and distant as they locked onto Sophie. There was no hint of the vulnerability he had shown her the night before. Only the cold, calculating man she had first met.

"You really think you can just defy me?" His voice was low, laced with a quiet rage that sent a chill down Sophie's spine.

Sophie held her ground, her gaze never wavering. "I don't know what you're doing, Alexander. I don't know what you've done to Emma. But I'm not going to let you hurt her."

His lips curled into a humorless smile. "You don't know what you're talking about. You never have." His eyes flickered to Emma, who was still hidden behind Sophie, her small form shaking. "And you don't understand the consequences of your actions."

Sophie's heart beat wildly in her chest. "What do you mean?" she demanded, her voice rising. "What consequences? What is happening here?"

Alexander took a step closer, his expression darkening. "The consequences of **betraying me**, Sophie," he said softly, his voice dangerously calm. "You think you can just walk in here and fix things? You think you can change everything with a few kind words?"

Sophie's stomach twisted. "I'm not trying to change anything. I'm just trying to keep her safe."

He moved even closer, and Sophie could feel the air between them growing heavier, thicker with every word. "Safety isn't something I can just hand out. It's something you earn. And you've done nothing to earn my trust." His eyes turned cold, and his gaze fixed on Emma again. "You're **out of your depth**, Sophie. And now, you've dragged Emma into your mess."

Sophie's mind spun. She didn't understand. She didn't know what game Alexander was playing, but she knew that it was more dangerous than anything she had anticipated. She wanted to push him, to demand answers, but something in his eyes told her that it was already too late. She was already trapped in his world.

"Please," Sophie whispered, her voice trembling with raw emotion. "I'm just trying to help her."

Alexander stared at her for a long moment, his face unreadable. Then, with a slight shake of his head, he turned away. "Help her? You can't help her, Sophie. You can't help any of us. You're just a temporary fix. A momentary distraction."

He paused, his back to her now. "And when the time comes, you'll be just like everyone else."

Before Sophie could respond, Alexander disappeared through the door, leaving her standing there, alone with Emma.

The room was silent except for the faint sound of Emma's breathing. Sophie felt the weight of everything pressing down on her—the **truth** she wasn't yet ready to understand, the dangers that were closing in around them, and the terrifying realization that she had just **unleashed** something she couldn't put back.

Sophie knew one thing for certain: She had no choice but to **fight**.

Sixteen

Unraveling Threads

The night had fallen heavy and oppressive, its weight almost suffocating. Sophie stood still in the library, the shadows from the dimly lit sconces stretching across the marble floors like reaching fingers. Emma sat on the plush armchair in the corner, her small form curled into itself, her eyes wide but empty. She hadn't spoken since Alexander's departure, her lips pressed tightly together in a way that made Sophie's heart ache.

Sophie tried to process everything that had just happened—the chilling confrontation with Alexander, his cryptic threats, and the way Emma had reacted to his presence. She could feel the unease gnawing at her insides, that sense that the world around her was beginning to collapse, piece by piece. Nothing was as it seemed. Nothing in the house was real, except the danger that loomed at every corner.

The door to the library creaked open, breaking the silence. Sophie's breath caught in her throat, but it was only Mrs. Laurent, standing in the doorway with her customary stern expression, her eyes cold as ice.

"You shouldn't be here," Mrs. Laurent said, her voice low but firm. "Mr. Wolfe is expecting you. You've made your point."

Sophie's pulse quickened, but she didn't back down. She couldn't afford to. "I'm not going anywhere," she said, her voice steady despite the storm raging in her chest. "Not until I know what's really going on. Not until I know what you've done to Emma."

Mrs. Laurent didn't flinch. "You have no idea what you're talking about," she said, her words laced with a warning. "You've seen enough to know that your place here is temporary, Sophie. And you've made your choice to interfere with things that should be left alone. But you should know something: there are consequences. Real consequences."

Sophie's breath hitched, her throat tightening as Mrs. Laurent stepped closer, the words hanging in the air between them. The warning was clear—there was something bigger at play here, something far darker than Sophie could understand. And yet, the more she pushed, the more she realized she was playing a game where the rules were being rewritten as they went along. Her every move felt like it was being watched, evaluated, and soon to be punished.

"I'm not afraid of your threats, Mrs. Laurent," Sophie said, her voice stronger now. "I don't care about your power games. I'm here for Emma, and I'll do whatever it takes to protect her."

Mrs. Laurent's lips curled into a cold smile, but her eyes betrayed something deeper. "You should be afraid, Miss Carter. You're not just dealing with me or with Mr. Wolfe. There are things that go beyond this house, beyond the walls of this estate. Things you can't even begin to imagine."

Sophie's blood ran cold, the hairs on the back of her neck standing up. There was something more—something sinister—that was controlling everything. She had sensed it the moment she walked into this house, but now the truth was beginning to unfurl in a way that felt impossible to ignore. Sophie wasn't just in a house filled with power and wealth. She was trapped in the web of something far darker, something that might tear her apart if she wasn't careful.

Emma's voice broke through the tension in the room. "Please... don't let them take me."

Sophie turned sharply, her heart breaking as she saw the fear in Emma's eyes—fear so raw it almost suffocated her. Sophie moved quickly to Emma's side, kneeling down to look her in the eye. "I won't let anyone hurt you, I promise," she said softly, trying to reassure the girl despite the storm inside her own heart. "But you need to tell me the truth, Emma. What's really going on? What did your father mean by 'consequences'?"

Emma hesitated, her lips trembling as she glanced at Mrs. Laurent, who stood in the doorway watching them. Sophie's eyes flicked between them, but Emma's gaze remained locked on the ground.

"They won't stop until they have what they want," Emma whispered, her voice barely audible. "They control everything. They make the rules, and they own everyone. You... you're just here because they want you to be. They let you stay because they need you for something."

Sophie's heart twisted as she processed Emma's words. She wasn't just a nanny—she was a tool, a pawn in a game she didn't fully understand. But that wasn't the worst part. The worst part was realizing that Emma had known this all along. She had been raised in this world of manipulation and control. The walls Emma had built around herself weren't just defenses; they were her survival mechanism.

Sophie shook her head, not willing to believe it. "But I'm here to protect you, Emma. You're just a child. You shouldn't have to live like this."

Emma's eyes were dark with fear. "You don't know who my father really is," she whispered, the weight of her words sinking into Sophie's bones like lead. "You don't know what he's done."

Before Sophie could respond, the door slammed open again, this time with force. The sound echoed in the room, and Sophie's heart leapt into her throat as Alexander stepped inside, his presence as overwhelming as ever. His gaze was cold, calculating, and yet there was something in his eyes that Sophie couldn't quite read—a mixture of something dark, something painful.

"You're making a mistake, Sophie," he said, his voice low, full of warning. "I don't want to hurt you. But you're pushing me into a corner. And that's not a place I like to be."

Sophie stood, her legs trembling beneath her, but her resolve firm. "I'm not afraid of you, Alexander," she said, her voice a little shaky but strong. "I'm not afraid of your threats."

He took a step forward, his eyes never leaving hers. There was no warmth, no comfort in his gaze—just cold, unfeeling calculation. "You should be," he said quietly. "This isn't just about you or Emma. This is about control. This is about making sure the world stays the way it should."

Sophie's heart raced. "What do you mean? What do you want from me?"

Alexander's lips curled into a small, dangerous smile. "I don't want anything from you, Sophie. But you're already involved. You've been involved since the moment you stepped into this house."

Sophie's mind raced, trying to piece together what he was saying. She was involved, but in what? She was just a nanny—just someone who had come to take care of Emma. She had no idea what kind of game Alexander was playing, but the danger was unmistakable now. She was more than just a bystander. She was part of this web, and there was no easy way out.

Before she could speak, the door behind Alexander opened, and a tall man stepped inside—someone Sophie had never seen before. He was dressed in a dark suit, his face impassive, his eyes scanning the room with a quiet intensity. He wasn't someone who belonged at a gala. He was someone else—someone who worked in the shadows, hidden from the public eye.

"Mr. Wolfe," the man said, his voice cold and measured. "The board is getting impatient. They're asking for an answer."

Alexander's eyes narrowed slightly, but his face remained unreadable. "I know," he said. "Tell them to wait. I'll handle it."

The man nodded, his gaze flickering over to Sophie and Emma before he stepped back out of the room, closing the door quietly behind him.

Sophie's pulse was pounding in her ears, the room feeling smaller with every passing second. The weight of what she had just heard settled over her like a thick fog, suffocating her with its implications. The board. Whoever these people were, whatever this business was, it was much bigger than she had imagined. Sophie wasn't just caught in a family's struggle for control; she was caught in something institutional, something far-reaching.

"Who are they?" Sophie whispered, her voice shaking. "Who's the board?"

Alexander didn't answer immediately. He stepped closer to her, his gaze never leaving hers. "People who make the world turn, Sophie," he said, his voice almost bored. "People who don't care about you, about Emma. They care about the future. They care about power."

Sophie's heart skipped. "And you're doing this for them? For power?"

Alexander's lips twitched slightly, but there was no humor in it. "I'm doing this for survival," he said quietly. "Power is what keeps us alive, Sophie. It's what keeps everything in motion. Without it, we'd all fall apart."

Sophie stared at him, her mind reeling. Everything she had suspected—the whispers, the tension, the strange, cold power that surrounded this family—was true. But it was bigger than she had ever imagined. This wasn't just a family in crisis. This was a dynasty, a machine, that ran on power, control, and manipulation.

She wasn't just fighting to protect Emma anymore. She was fighting to survive.

And as she looked into Alexander's cold eyes, Sophie realized that the game had never been just about her. She had become a pawn in a much bigger, more dangerous game than she could ever have imagined.

And the real game was just beginning.

Seventeen

The Breaking Point

Sophie stood frozen, the weight of Alexander's words sinking in like a stone in her stomach. She had walked into this house thinking she was simply taking a job—a nanny, someone who would care for a troubled little girl and maybe, just maybe, make a difference. But now, standing in front of Alexander, she realized how naïve she had been. This wasn't just a job. It was a trap, and she had been caught in the snare the moment she stepped foot in the Wolfe estate.

The door clicked softly behind her, the quiet noise snapping her back to reality. Alexander's presence loomed over her, almost suffocating in its intensity. His eyes, sharp and calculating, never left hers, and Sophie could feel the pressure mounting with every second they stood there in silence. His earlier words—about power, about survival—had shaken her more than she cared to admit. Sophie had always thought she understood the world of the rich, the powerful. She had spent years working for families like the Wolfes, but nothing had prepared her for this. For him.

Emma sat in the corner, still trembling, her wide eyes watching them both, but she said nothing. Sophie didn't have the luxury of being weak, of showing fear. She couldn't afford to fall apart—not in front of Emma, not in front of Alexander.

But she was starting to feel it—the breaking point was close. The tension, the constant sense of being watched, of being part of a game she didn't understand, was suffocating. The longer she stayed here, the more she realized how deep the web of control really went. And how dangerous the people at the center of it were.

"You think you can just walk away from this?" Alexander's voice cut through the silence, his words like ice against her skin. "You think you can walk into this house, into my life, and change things?"

Sophie's pulse raced, but she forced herself to stand tall, to stare back at him. "I don't think I'm changing anything," she said, her voice steadier than she felt. "But I'm not going to sit here and watch you destroy this little girl."

A flicker of something—something unreadable—flashed across Alexander's face. For a brief second, it almost seemed like he was about to say something, but he stopped himself. Instead, he walked across the room, his movements deliberate, almost as though he was trying to own the space.

The Breaking Point

Sophie's gaze followed him, her instincts screaming at her to be cautious. Every fiber of her being told her to be careful. This was not the man she had hoped he was. The vulnerable man who had shared pieces of his past, the one who seemed to care about his daughter—that version of Alexander was gone. In his place stood someone cold, manipulative, someone who would stop at nothing to maintain his control over his world.

He stopped at the window, his back to her, staring out at the darkened estate beyond. "You have no idea what I've built," he said quietly, almost to himself. "You have no idea the things I've done to protect this family." His voice hardened. "And now you want to undo it all."

Sophie stepped closer, her hand clenched at her side. "I don't want to undo anything," she said firmly. "But Emma doesn't deserve this. She doesn't deserve to be raised in this world of fear, of manipulation."

Alexander's shoulders stiffened, and when he turned to face her, his eyes were cold, like shards of glass. "You think you know what she deserves? You think you know what she needs?" He took a step toward her, his presence overwhelming. "You don't know what she needs, Sophie. You have no idea what it's like to live in my world, to survive in this house."

The words hit Sophie like a physical blow, and for a moment, she was caught off guard. He was right in some ways. She had no idea what it was like to live in his world. To be forced into a life of constant control, where everything was calculated, every move watched. But that didn't mean she couldn't see the damage it was doing. She didn't need to be part of it to understand the consequences of this kind of power.

"Your world is broken, Alexander," she said softly. "And so is Emma's. She's just a little girl, but you're teaching her how to live in fear. She doesn't know how to trust anyone."

Alexander's eyes darkened, his jaw tightening. "Trust is for the weak," he spat, his voice low and threatening. "Trust doesn't keep you alive in this world. Power does."

Sophie's stomach churned at the venom in his voice, but she stood her ground. "You're wrong. Power doesn't keep people alive. It destroys them. It destroys everything that's good inside them. And it's destroying Emma."

He took another step closer to her, his face now just inches from hers. Sophie's breath hitched, the weight of his gaze pinning her in place. "You think I'm the problem?" he murmured, his voice deceptively calm. "You think that I'm the one destroying her? You don't know anything about what I've done, Sophie. You don't know what it's like to be in my shoes."

Sophie's eyes flashed with defiance. "I don't care about your excuses, Alexander. I'm not going to let you manipulate her. I'm not going to stand by and watch her become another part of your empire of fear."

For a long moment, there was silence. The air between them seemed to crackle with tension, thick with the unsaid words that hung heavy in the room. And then, with a sudden movement, Alexander stepped back, his eyes hardening into something unreadable.

"You're making a mistake, Sophie," he said, his voice cold. "You don't understand who you're dealing with."

"I understand perfectly," she said, her voice unwavering. "You're just a man hiding behind his power. And you've dragged your daughter into this world of darkness."

Alexander's gaze softened for a fraction of a second, but it was quickly replaced by something far colder. He turned sharply, his voice laced with something dangerous. "You're already too involved. And that will be your downfall."

Before Sophie could respond, the door to the library opened again, and Mrs. Laurent stepped inside. Her presence was like a shadow falling over the room, a cold reminder of who truly held the power in this house.

"Mr. Wolfe," Mrs. Laurent said, her voice dripping with formality. "The board is asking for an update. They're becoming impatient."

Alexander didn't look at her. He didn't need to. He just turned and gave her a barely perceptible nod, as though everything was already decided.

"Take her," he said flatly, his gaze flicking to Sophie one last time. "Take her back to the ballroom. Make sure she knows her place."

Sophie felt the blood rush to her face, a hot wave of anger flooding her chest. He was banishing her again. Dismissing her as if she were nothing more than a servant. But it wasn't just her he was dismissing. It was Emma, too. It was their entire future that Alexander was threatening, all for the sake of his precious control.

Mrs. Laurent moved toward her with a swift, efficient motion, her hands gripping Sophie's arm with enough force to make her wince. "You've made your point, Miss Carter," she said coldly. "Now come with me. The night is far from over."

Sophie stood still for a moment, her pulse pounding in her ears. She had never felt more trapped in her life. She wanted to fight. She wanted to scream, to break free from this prison of lies and manipulation. But deep down, Sophie knew that if she didn't play by their rules, if she didn't conform, there would be no way out.

She glanced back at Emma, whose eyes were still wide with fear. Sophie's heart clenched. She couldn't leave the girl like this. She couldn't just give up.

"Emma," she whispered, her voice filled with raw emotion. "I promise I'm not going anywhere. I'm going to make sure you're safe. I'll always be here for you."

Emma didn't respond, but the faintest flicker of something—hope?—flashed across her face before it disappeared, buried beneath the layers of fear that had built up over the years.

The Breaking Point

With one final glance at Emma, Sophie followed Mrs. Laurent out of the library, her mind a whirlwind of thoughts. She had made her decision. There was no going back now. The world she had stepped into was dark and dangerous, but Sophie knew one thing for sure: she wasn't going to let Alexander Wolfe destroy Emma—not without a fight.

As the heavy door of the ballroom swung open before her, Sophie stepped inside, her heart pounding. The night was far from over, and neither was her battle.

Eighteen

Into the Fire

Sophie's footsteps echoed through the grand hallway, the sound a haunting reminder of how alone she felt in this suffocating mansion. Every step she took seemed to bring her closer to something she couldn't quite grasp—something dangerous, something she wasn't ready for. The weight of her decision to confront Alexander, to fight for Emma, seemed heavier with each passing second. She had crossed a line, yes—but in this house, lines were drawn in the sand only to be washed away by the tide of power, money, and control.

Mrs. Laurent's grip on Sophie's arm was like a vice, unyielding and cold. There was no warmth, no sympathy in the woman's eyes. She moved with a precision that suggested years of practice in maintaining control, and Sophie felt the sharpness of it, the unspoken message: You are not welcome here anymore. As they walked back toward the ballroom, the lights of the chandelier above flickered like distant stars—beautiful, but unreachable.

When they reached the ballroom, Sophie's stomach churned. The noise of the guests—their laughter, their clinking glasses—felt like a distant, muffled roar, drowning out her thoughts. She had never felt so out of place in a room full of people who should have been her peers. But they weren't her peers. They were predators, and Sophie was just a pawn in their game.

Mrs. Laurent finally released Sophie's arm, though she didn't leave her side. Her presence was a constant reminder of the rules of this world, rules Sophie was beginning to understand all too well. She would never be allowed to leave this place, not unless she played along. And Emma? What would happen to Emma? Would the girl ever truly escape the suffocating grip of her father's world?

Sophie felt the eyes of the guests turn toward her as she stepped into the ballroom, and a surge of anxiety hit her. The room felt colder somehow, though the heat of the summer night outside should have made it feel like a sanctuary. Instead, it felt like a prison—a gilded cage made of silk and gold.

"Miss Carter, there you are." The voice that cut through the crowd wasn't familiar, but it had the smooth, dangerous edge that Sophie had come to associate with the wealthy and powerful. She turned slowly, her heart in her throat.

Standing before her was Jonathan Hargrave, the man she had

seen talking to Alexander earlier. He was dressed impeccably in a dark suit, his hands resting casually in his pockets. But his smile, though charming, didn't reach his eyes. There was a coldness to him, a calculating coldness that sent a shiver down Sophie's spine.

"Mr. Hargrave," Sophie said, forcing a polite smile. "I didn't realize you were expecting me."

Hargrave chuckled, a low, dark sound that sent an uncomfortable ripple through the air. "Expecting? No. But I always like to meet the new additions to the family. Mr. Wolfe has… quite the interesting taste in company."

Sophie stiffened at the implication. She had known it would come to this—the whispers, the subtle insinuations. She had already become part of the rumor mill, a tool for gossip in a world where everything was a game.

"I'm just here to do my job, Mr. Hargrave," Sophie replied coolly, trying to keep her voice steady despite the rising anger inside her. "Nothing more, nothing less."

Hargrave's eyes gleamed, as if he were enjoying this little verbal duel. "Of course," he said smoothly, stepping closer to her. His cologne wafted through the air, thick and overpowering. "But tell me, Miss Carter—do you really think you can just walk into Mr. Wolfe's world and leave unscathed?"

Sophie's stomach twisted. She knew exactly what he was implying, and it didn't sit well with her. Hargrave was no stranger to danger. He was a man who thrived in the shadows, who made deals that no one else would dare to touch. And she had just made the mistake of stepping into his world, unprepared for the consequences.

Before she could answer, she felt a hand rest lightly on her shoulder, sending a jolt of electricity through her spine. She turned sharply to find Alexander standing behind her, his gaze dark and unreadable.

"Jonathan," he said in a tone that was smooth, almost cordial, but there was an edge to it that Sophie immediately recognized. "I see you've made Miss Carter's acquaintance."

Hargrave's eyes gleamed as he nodded, stepping back to give Alexander space. "Just a little chat," he said, his voice dripping with faux sincerity. "Making sure she knows the rules of the game."

Alexander didn't acknowledge Hargrave's words, instead focusing solely on Sophie. His eyes locked onto hers with an intensity that almost made her breath catch. She could feel the pressure of his gaze, the weight of his expectations. He wasn't just a man to be feared—he was a man who could manipulate, control, and destroy with the flick of his wrist.

"I've had enough of this," Alexander said, his voice low, his eyes flicking toward the crowd of guests still watching them. "We need to talk. Now."

Before Sophie could protest, he took her arm—gently but

firmly—and began to pull her toward the side doors, away from the main ballroom. She didn't have the option to resist. There was no chance to fight, no way to walk away. She had already been marked, already drawn into his world, and now, there was no escaping it.

As they stepped through the side door and into a quieter corridor, Sophie's breath quickened, her chest tightening. The silence was suffocating, and the tension between them felt like it was cracking. Sophie wanted to lash out, wanted to demand answers, but she held her tongue, knowing that pushing him now would only make things worse.

Alexander stopped once they were out of sight from the ballroom, his back turned to her as he stared out of the window. The moonlight illuminated his features, casting long shadows across his face. Sophie couldn't tell if the distance between them was intentional or if it was simply how he operated—always in control, always looking down at everyone beneath him.

"You don't understand what you're dealing with," Alexander said after a long moment, his voice low and dangerous.

Sophie's breath caught in her throat. "I think I understand perfectly," she replied, her voice trembling despite her best efforts to sound strong. "This isn't just about Emma, is it? This is about you. You control everything, you make the rules, and you want to make sure no one can ever challenge you."

Alexander didn't turn to look at her, but his posture stiffened.

"You have no idea," he said, his voice a whisper in the night. "You think this is about control. But it's not. It's about survival."

Sophie stepped closer, her eyes narrowing. "Survival? You think that controlling everyone around you—destroying everything good in your life—is survival?"

He finally turned to face her, and there it was again—that look—the cold, empty gaze that told her everything. He was broken, buried beneath layers of power and self-preservation.

"You think I'm the one who's broken?" he asked quietly. "You think you're the one who can fix this? Fix me?"

Sophie's heart twisted in her chest. "I'm not trying to fix you," she said softly, her voice filled with something raw. "I'm trying to save Emma."

Alexander's eyes flashed. "Emma is already lost," he said, his words biting through the air. "She's trapped in a world of my making. And there's nothing you can do to change that."

Sophie recoiled at the harshness in his tone, but she refused to back down. "She's just a child, Alexander. She deserves to live, to feel. You've stripped her of everything—her innocence, her hope."

Alexander's gaze softened for a brief moment, but it was quickly replaced by something darker, more calculating. "You have no idea what I've sacrificed to get here," he said. "To keep her safe. To protect everything I've built. I've had to make choices—hard choices. And if you're not willing to understand that, Sophie, you won't survive here."

Sophie's heart skipped in her chest. "Survive? What are you saying, Alexander?"

He stepped closer, his face only inches from hers now. She could feel the heat of his breath, the electricity in the air between them. "I'm saying you need to make a decision, Sophie," he said, his voice dangerously quiet. "Are you going to continue being part of this game, or are you going to walk away? But if you choose to stay, you'd better understand that the consequences will follow you."

The words hung in the air, suffocating and ominous. Sophie felt trapped, caught in the web of a game she didn't want to play. Her eyes searched his face, looking for any sign of the man she had seen those few days ago—the man who had shown her vulnerability, who had opened up about his past. But all she saw now was a man consumed by power, by fear, by something darker than she could comprehend.

"I'm not afraid of your threats," Sophie said, her voice breaking through the tension. "I'll fight for Emma. I'll fight for what's right."

Alexander's lips curled into a smirk, and for the first time, Sophie felt something truly terrifying: the calm before the storm.

"Then prepare yourself, Sophie," he said softly. "The storm is already here."

As he turned away, Sophie's stomach twisted with a sense of dread that no words could quell. She was deep in the heart of the storm, and she had no idea how long she could survive it.

Nineteen

The Fall

Sophie stood in the darkened hallway, her pulse still pounding from her last conversation with Alexander. His words echoed in her mind, a haunting reminder of the choice she now faced. The storm was already here. The game had changed, and Sophie had no idea how to play it.

She pressed her back against the cold, marble wall, her breath coming in shallow bursts as she tried to steady herself. The house felt colder now, the silence pressing in on her from all sides, wrapping around her like a suffocating blanket. The ballroom, with its gleaming lights and laughter, felt like a distant memory now. The harsh reality of Alexander's world had swallowed her whole, and there was no turning back.

Sophie glanced down the corridor. The house seemed to stretch on endlessly, its winding halls and dark corners hiding

The Fall

more secrets than she could begin to unravel. But it was Emma who mattered now. The child she had promised to protect. Sophie's gaze flickered back toward the library, where Emma was still waiting, her fragile form a constant reminder of the weight Sophie now carried on her shoulders.

Sophie could feel the heat of the tears that threatened to spill from her eyes, but she refused to let them fall. Not yet. Not in this house. This was no time for weakness. She had to be strong for Emma. She had to be the one to hold it all together. But the truth was, she didn't know how much longer she could keep pretending that she had control over anything. The walls of this mansion were closing in on her, and there were forces at play that she couldn't even begin to understand.

The sudden sound of footsteps behind her made her heart skip a beat. She turned quickly, her breath catching in her throat. But it wasn't Alexander. It was Mrs. Laurent.

The woman's expression was as cold and emotionless as ever, her eyes narrowing slightly as she took in Sophie's disheveled appearance. There was no warmth in the way she looked at her—no sympathy. Just the same quiet judgment that Sophie had come to expect from her.

"Mr. Wolfe is waiting for you," Mrs. Laurent said, her voice clipped and formal. "You should not keep him waiting."

Sophie's chest tightened at the mention of Alexander. She had known this moment would come. She had known that eventually, she would be summoned back to him. But something about the way Mrs. Laurent spoke, the underlying tension in her voice, made Sophie's stomach churn. She wasn't just being called back to speak with Alexander—she was being summoned into the lion's den.

Sophie took a deep breath, trying to steady her nerves. "I'm not going anywhere until I know what's going on with Emma," she said, her voice steady but filled with a quiet resolve. "You can tell Mr. Wolfe that."

Mrs. Laurent's lips curled into a small smile, but it wasn't a smile that reached her eyes. "You think you have a choice in this, Miss Carter?" she asked softly, her voice laced with mockery. "You're already involved. You've been involved from the moment you stepped into this house. You don't get to walk away now."

Sophie flinched at the venom in Mrs. Laurent's words, but she didn't back down. She had no intention of being manipulated any further. She had already crossed a line—there was no turning back now.

"I'm staying with Emma," Sophie said, her voice firm. "I won't be part of your game, Mrs. Laurent. And I won't let you take her back into whatever nightmare you've created for her."

The woman's smile faltered, but it returned just as quickly. "You're not in control here, Miss Carter. You never were." She stepped closer, her presence cold and imposing. "You've made a choice, whether you realize it or not. And now you'll face the consequences."

The Fall

The weight of her words hung heavy in the air, and for a moment, Sophie felt the full weight of the threat that Mrs. Laurent was implying. She had thought she was in control, thought that she could protect Emma and shield her from the dangers lurking in this house. But now, standing face-to-face with this woman, Sophie realized just how far she had fallen into the trap. She was trapped, and there was no way out. Not unless she was willing to fight for everything she believed in.

"Fine," Sophie said, her voice steady despite the surge of fear rising in her chest. "If I have to face the consequences, then so be it. But I won't stop fighting for Emma."

Mrs. Laurent's lips twitched, but she didn't say another word. Instead, she turned on her heel and walked back toward the ballroom, leaving Sophie standing alone in the dimly lit corridor. Her words lingered in the air, a chilling reminder of the game she was playing. Sophie's heart was heavy with the knowledge that she was being pulled deeper into something that might destroy her.

But she wasn't going to back down. Not now. Not when Emma's safety was on the line.

Sophie walked toward the library, her steps slow but purposeful. As she pushed open the door, her eyes immediately found Emma, still sitting in the same armchair. The girl looked up as Sophie entered, her eyes wide and fearful.

"Are you okay?" Sophie asked softly, walking over to the chair and kneeling beside Emma. She placed a gentle hand on the girl's trembling arm, trying to offer some comfort, but the child flinched away from her touch.

"I don't want to go back," Emma whispered, her voice barely audible. "I don't want to go back there. I'm scared."

Sophie's heart broke at the sight of Emma's fear. The girl had been through more than anyone should have to endure in their lifetime. And yet, here she was, still fighting, still clinging to some semblance of hope. Sophie knew she couldn't let her down now.

"You don't have to go back, Emma," Sophie said softly, her voice filled with fierce determination. "I'm not going to let them take you. We'll figure this out together. I promise you."

Emma looked up at her, her eyes filled with desperation. "But he'll make me. He always does."

Sophie's stomach twisted. He. Emma was talking about Alexander. The man who had destroyed so many things in her life, the man who had made her believe that there was no escape from his control. But Sophie wasn't going to let that happen—not to Emma, not to herself.

"We'll fight him," Sophie said firmly, her voice steady. "We'll find a way out. I won't let him control you anymore, Emma. You deserve a chance to live your life, to be a child."

Emma's face crumpled in a mixture of fear and hope, and Sophie felt her heart break all over again. But she couldn't

The Fall

show weakness. Not now. Not when Emma needed her the most.

Sophie took a deep breath and stood, holding out her hand to Emma. "Come on," she said gently. "We're not alone in this. We'll get through it."

Emma hesitated for a moment, her eyes searching Sophie's face as if trying to read her. And then, slowly, she reached out, her small hand trembling as it met Sophie's.

The moment their hands touched, a wave of resolve washed over Sophie. She couldn't back down. She couldn't let Alexander win. She would fight for Emma, for her safety, for her future, no matter what it took.

As they walked toward the door, Sophie's mind raced. She had to confront Alexander—she had to stand up to him and demand answers. She had to protect Emma, even if it meant risking everything. The fight for Emma's freedom was just beginning, and Sophie knew that the battle was going to be harder and more dangerous than anything she had ever faced.

But she wasn't afraid anymore. Because no matter what, she was going to win.

They stepped into the hallway, and for the first time since she had arrived in this house, Sophie didn't feel like she was drowning. She felt like she had found her purpose, and with it, the strength to face whatever came next. The storm was far from over, but Sophie was ready. She was ready to fight.

Twenty

The Reckoning

The cold hallway stretched before Sophie like a vast, empty ocean, and she could feel every step they took reverberate through her chest. The weight of her decision pressed heavily on her, the sense of foreboding thick in the air. Her fingers curled tightly around Emma's hand, the child's small fingers trembling slightly, but Sophie's grip was firm. She wouldn't let go. Not now. Not ever.

The shadows of the mansion seemed to close in on them as they walked, each passing corner feeling like another trap. She could hear the distant sound of the party still going on in the ballroom behind her, the laughter and music muffled by the walls, as if the world outside was oblivious to the tension building in this house. But Sophie knew. She knew something was about to break.

The Reckoning

They reached the door leading to Alexander's study, a place Sophie had only been in once, and the air around her grew heavier. The study was where Alexander retreated when he needed to make decisions. The place where he controlled everything—his world, his empire—and Sophie knew that soon, very soon, she would have to face him there.

Sophie stopped just before the door, her heart thudding in her chest. She could feel the presence of power behind that door, the dark energy that hung like a storm cloud over everything. Her pulse quickened, but she didn't let herself falter. She couldn't afford to. Not for Emma. Not for herself.

Emma, sensing the shift in energy, looked up at her with wide, fearful eyes. Sophie crouched down, meeting her gaze.

"I'm here," Sophie said, her voice soft but steady. "I'm not going anywhere. Whatever happens next, we'll face it together."

Emma nodded, but Sophie could see the hesitation in her eyes. She was just a child, but in many ways, Emma had already been forced to grow up far too quickly. Sophie couldn't begin to imagine what this life had done to her—what Alexander had done to her.

The door to the study loomed in front of them, a dark portal into a world Sophie had only begun to understand. She reached for the handle, her breath shallow, and pushed it open.

The study was quiet. Too quiet. The room was large, dimly lit by the soft glow of desk lamps and the faint light filtering through the tall windows. The rich, dark wood of the bookshelves seemed to absorb the light, casting long shadows across the floor. The air was thick with the smell of leather-bound books and cigars—an aroma that felt both intimate and forbidding.

At the far end of the room, standing by the large desk that dominated the space, was Alexander. His back was to them, and Sophie could hear the faint sound of paper being shuffled, as if he were deliberately ignoring them, giving them time to gather their courage.

She stepped forward, Emma close behind her, and Alexander turned slowly. His eyes were cold, calculating—completely unreadable—but there was something else beneath that hardness, something raw that Sophie could almost feel in the air. It was the same darkness she had seen in him before, the darkness that drove him to control everything around him.

"You've made your choice, then," he said, his voice smooth, but there was a tightness to it. His eyes flicked from Sophie to Emma, a flicker of something Sophie couldn't quite decipher passing through his gaze. "You've chosen to stand in my way. To challenge me."

Sophie's heart hammered in her chest, but she held her ground. "I'm not here to challenge you, Alexander," she said, her voice clear and unwavering. "I'm here to protect Emma. I'm here to make sure she's not another pawn in your game."

Alexander's lips curled into a tight, humorless smile, and he took a step toward her. "You think I don't know what's best for her? You think you can just waltz in here and tell me what I should be doing with my daughter?"

His voice was low, barely a whisper, but it cut through Sophie's resolve like a knife. He didn't care. He didn't care about Emma. He didn't care about anyone but himself and his need for control.

Sophie took a deep breath, her fingers tightening around Emma's hand. "You don't get it, do you?" she asked, her voice shaking slightly. "You've taken everything from her. Her childhood. Her innocence. She's not some asset for you to manipulate and control, Alexander. She's a little girl. She deserves a chance to be happy."

The smile faded from his face, and for a moment, Sophie saw something else—a flicker of emotion, fleeting and barely perceptible, like a crack in the icy facade he had built around himself. It was gone before she could register it, replaced by that cold, calculating gaze. But for just a second, Sophie could feel the weight of his conflict.

"You don't understand the world I live in, Sophie," he said, his voice low and dangerous. "You don't understand the pressures I face every single day. You don't understand what it takes to keep this family safe. To keep us safe."

Sophie stepped closer, her gaze unwavering. "Safety isn't what you think it is," she said. "You can't keep Emma safe by burying her under layers of control and fear. You're suffocating her."

Alexander's fists clenched at his sides, his jaw tightening. "You have no idea what I've sacrificed for her," he spat. "You have no idea what I've done to make sure she doesn't become a victim. Everything I've done, every choice I've made, has been to keep her from the world's cruelty."

Sophie shook her head slowly, her voice breaking through the walls he had built around himself. "No, Alexander. You're not keeping her from cruelty. You're just teaching her to be afraid. Afraid of everything."

For a moment, there was silence. The tension between them was thick, like the air just before a storm. Sophie could feel the weight of it, could feel the suffocating pressure that came with being in this room with him. But she didn't back down. She couldn't.

"I won't let you destroy her," Sophie said, her voice quiet but filled with fierce resolve. "I'll fight for her, Alexander. I'll fight for her freedom. I won't let you take away what's left of her soul."

Alexander's eyes flashed with anger, but then something changed. A deep, almost inhuman calm seemed to settle over him. He turned away from Sophie, walking toward his desk, his movements deliberate. He picked up a thick folder of papers and opened it slowly, as if the weight of the moment was somehow beneath him.

Sophie's breath caught in her throat. What was he doing?

"You think you can fight me," he said, his voice so cold it sent a shiver down Sophie's spine. "But you're just one person. And no matter how hard you try, you'll never be able to fight what I've built. You'll never be able to break me. You'll never be able to take her from me."

Sophie stepped forward, her voice trembling but determined. "I don't care how much power you have. I'll fight with everything I have to protect Emma. Even if it means facing you."

Alexander didn't respond. He didn't need to. The finality in his gaze was enough. He was done with the conversation. Sophie knew that. And the moment she had feared, the moment she had been dreading, was finally upon them.

"You're not going to win this," he said, his voice quiet, almost to himself. "No one does. You'll learn that soon enough."

With a final glance, Alexander turned his back to them, walking toward the large window that overlooked the estate. He was done with them. But Sophie wasn't done. Not by a long shot.

She turned to Emma, who had been silent the entire time, watching with wide, terrified eyes. Sophie knelt down in front of her, brushing a strand of hair from her face. "We're going to get out of here," Sophie whispered, her voice filled with promise. "I won't stop until you're free."

But deep down, she knew it wasn't going to be easy. The storm had just begun, and the reckoning was far from over.

www.ingramcontent.com/pod-product-compliance
Lightning Source LLC
LaVergne TN
LVHW011945070526
838202LV00054B/4804